STUCK

STUCK

A WAY OUT

KIM CASEY COBB

Clovercroft Publishing

Stuck

Published by Clovercroft Publishing, Franklin, Tennessee

Edited by Lee Titus Elliott

Cover Design by Nelly Sanchez

Interior Design by Adept Content Solutions

Printed in the United States of America

ISBN   978-1-948484-73-2

This book is dedicated to my mother,
Laquita, and my brother, Tim.

Contents

Acknowledgments

First and foremost, I would like to say "thank you" to my husband, Darrell. Thank you for seeing the real me. Your unconditional love and support for the things I want to accomplish has been so important to me. You hold the number one place in my life, and I will always love you more than anything or anyone. I could not have finished this book without you in my corner.

To my kids, Cody and Courtney, for accepting me so openly into your life, for allowing me to be a parent to you, and never treating me like anything less than a mom. Your presence and inspiration in my life helped open my eyes and create empathy towards my own mother, which had a direct impact on our reconciliation and subsequently developing a loving relationship.

To my friends: Julie, Angie, Carroll, Gail. For the consistent encouragement to tell my story and believing it was a story worth telling.

To the Moran family: the people I met through you that encouraged and assisted me in completing this book have been instrumental. The book would not be what it is without those connections.

Last but not least, to all of my mentors. You'll never know how much the opportunities to learn from you have meant.

Nothing is as painful as staying stuck
somewhere you don't belong.
—Mandy Hale

Chapter 1
Introduction

Have you ever noticed that when women succeed, they are more likely to attribute their success to luck and help from others, yet when they fail, they blame their own lack of ability? Why is that? More important, what can we do to change this?

Five years from now, you will be the same as you are today, except for the people you meet and the new things you expose yourself to. You Today + People You Meet + Things You Learn = Future You. You are also the average of five people you associate yourself with. Mediocrity breeds mediocrity.

I am a woman who has overcome adversity and chosen not to be a victim of my circumstances. I have taken responsibility for developing my abilities in order to keep moving forward in life. I am passionate about continuous learning, solving problems, believing I can make a difference, and seeing people I have mentored succeed. I am adamantly motivated to share my experiences and story with you. My sincere hope is that you will find some useful nuggets from my personal journey to apply to your own path forward.

I believe in a world of future possibilities. I believe that anything is possible with the right mentality and enough hard work, determination, willpower, and faith.

1

STUCK

I have been extremely moved to write this book because I believe that no matter where a person starts out in life, there is NO excuse for not making something of yourself. I want to share my story and the things that I have learned over the last thirty years that have helped me overcome adversity and succeed. I want to share that with others who may be struggling to move mountains in their own lives. Seeing others strive for and meet their own personal potential makes me incredibly happy. As a result, my passion has become to provide motivation to people to help them not only see their own potential and future possibilities but achieve them.

For women who are "stuck," I want to help free their minds and thoughts from the bondage of self-pity and lack of confidence. I want them to open up and see that the limits to what they can achieve exist only in their own minds. I want women to realize that those who empower themselves and self-educate, who are willing to devote some of their personal time to that effort and not wait on someone to bring it to them, are more successful and happy than those that sit on the sidelines drowning in self-pity with victim-like mentalities and complacency, all the while waiting on things to magically change.

If you embrace the mentality to continuously expand your knowledge through learning new things, then you will literally change your life, because it will continue to improve as you continue to learn.

When you realize YOU are in charge of whether your life stays the same or not, you understand that it isn't even possible to "go back" to what life was like last week, last month, or last year.

2

This mentality will set you on a course that will bring so many opportunities your way, which means you will continue to have more and more options for yourself and never be trapped. This, the exact opposite of stagnation, is true freedom. Growth in all areas of life becomes possible once you start managing your life this way.

This book is different than others you may read. I am and always have been frank, blunt, and even somewhat "tough love" with my style and the advice that I have to offer. You will find no sugarcoating in what I have to say. I accept no excuses from myself or others. Be assured that I speak the truth out of love and a desire to see people overcome adversity in their lives.

I will encourage you to eliminate the mental barriers that are holding you back and be aggressive in believing in yourself and your God-given abilities. I will show you how you can get on the path to accomplishment quickly with a shift in the way you think about and view yourself and your future, and I will expose options in life that have been buried under the weight of your present circumstances. You will learn to eliminate any sense of victimization and set down any self-blame that you may currently be carrying and turn your life around.

If you are a female, a young woman from a poor background, a woman starting over after a relationship, or a woman at a cross-roads in life, then this book is for you. If you feel "stuck" or as though you are not moving forward, then this book is for you. If you feel your life is out of control and you have no hope or options, then this book is for you.

People who know me today see a put-together, polished, confident, and successful person. There have been times I've been told by some of those I am attempting to mentor that it is impossible for them to achieve more than what they currently have because they weren't "given the same opportunities in life that I

3

was." I never accept this from anyone. Every day is an opportunity. That you are alive is an opportunity. If you knew where I started, you might not think it would have been possible to pull out of the muck and to form the life I have today.

The starting line of the race wasn't even visible from where I stood as a child.

I was the product of an extremely dysfunctional family, where unhealthy circumstances had been rolling into a giant snowball for generations. The situation erupted when I was nine years old and my noncustodial father abducted my younger brother and me from our mother in the middle of the night on a routine weekend visitation during their bitter divorce. Around midnight of one cold night in May of 1979, he woke us up, piled us in his little blue Subaru with nothing but the clothes on our backs, and drove away through the snow-covered mountain passes near Jackson Hole, Wyoming. As adults, we sometimes try to put our finger on the moment in time that set our destiny, plotted our course, or was the most significant over any other in our life. That day was a fork in the road of my family's life.

I became an official FBI missing person and one of the first kids on a milk carton. We lived in constant fear of being caught. We were not allowed to walk in front of cameras, and we made sure we turned and looked the other way when we saw a policeman. If we encountered one in the car on the road, Dad forced us to immediately hide on the floorboard, afraid we would be recognized. Posters were out all over the country with our pictures on them. Our photos and story were run in newspapers and on the radio, and our case was listed with the National Center for Missing and Exploited Children and Child Find. Although she never stopped trying, our mother was never able to find us.

In the beginning, we honestly did miss our mother, as children would. I wanted to talk to her. I remember that shortly after the abduction, we were hiding at my grandfather's house in Oklahoma, sitting at a table with my dad, looking at a map of the United States. He was trying to figure out where to take us next. I searched for and found the city and state where my mom was and kissed it, saying, "And a kiss for Mommy!" To which my dad replied, "Why do you want to kiss *her*?" During that time, I also walked in on him speaking to her on the phone, harassing her and telling her what he was going to do to her if she did not stop looking for us. I asked to talk to her, but he waved me away. I felt ashamed, as though I had done something wrong. My dad began sitting us down and talking to us about what a bad person our mother really was. He told us many things, such as she was going to take us from him by obtaining sole custody and not allowing him to see us at all. The perspective that we began to have was that in order for us to see our dad at all, we had no choice but to live in hiding with him. We began to defend him and quickly became angry with our mother for continuing to chase us. In our minds, it became her fault that we had to live on the run, as we were doing. It was an irrational mind-set that was perpetrated on my brother and me.

The situation became one of little hope to all of us. According to my dad and his radical paranoia, there were only two possible outcomes if my mom found us. Dad would either go to prison, where he would be subjected to the nightmarish treatment he envisioned in his mind, or he would be shot in cold blood in front of us by the "hit man" my mother had hired to kill him. He made it perfectly clear that he would rather be shot or take his own life than go to prison.

After living as homeless fugitives under assumed identities for years, I ran away at the age of sixteen . I did not finish high school. I obtained my high school diploma by taking my GED when I was eighteen. I escaped the oppression and control of my dad, thinking I was home free, and yet I allowed myself to backtrack into an unhealthy and abusive relationship with another man. I sank into a victim-like mentality and allowed myself to believe that I couldn't have what other "normal" people had because of what had happened to me. I mistakenly believed that the work necessary to produce the life I dreamed of and coveted was too hard. I eventually came out the other side and formed healthy relationships, met a wonderful man, gained a family, and have had a successful career. This was a result of continuously seeking the truth, soul searching, breaking free from mental strongholds, surrounding myself with the right people, and constantly feeding myself with knowledge and learning skills necessary to move forward in life.

After reading this book, you will understand that it is possible to get "unstuck." You will realize, "Yes, I can!" You will learn valuable mental strategies to move forward and propel yourself up and away from your current situation that is holding you back and move towards the inspired life you were meant to lead. It really is possible to move forward, and I'll show you how this is true, through telling my own story and helping you understand just how much you are in control of. I will help you define success for yourself and actually envision it becoming a reality in your life.

> Nothing is powerful enough to hold you back, unless you choose to allow it to do so.

Life has no remote; you have to get up and change it yourself. Life may not be fair, but this is true for everyone, so chasing "fairness" is never a reason to hold yourself back.

It's a fact that the same boiling water that softens a potato also hardens an egg. It's about what you are made of, not the circumstances you find yourself in. You are always stronger than you think you are, and in this book, we will work to destroy any dysfunctional belief systems that you may be clinging to. We will remove negative and harmful self-talk, lies you are telling yourself, or lies others have told you, and replace them with positive truths. Your new reality will emerge and, with it, a passion for what you can do in your life.

You will come to understand that you are confined only by the walls you build yourself. You will learn to think for yourself and not allow past or present sufferings to poison your view of the future. You will ask yourself these questions and answer them: What do I want? Why do I want it? How will I achieve it? You'll have all kinds of days on this journey, but every day you will show up, and you will see results.

You will come to understand that you will never find a better sparring partner than adversity. It is a tool you can use to become better and to grow into the person you were intended to be. As my mother likes to say,

> "It's not about what happened to us; it is about what we do with it."

This came from a woman who had her children ripped from her and who was not reunited with them until they were adults. I am going to show you how to do something amazing with the life circumstances you have either inherited or taken on yourself.

We will utilize techniques from the business world to help you get in tune with your true self, to establish conviction by identifying your values, to create a personal mission, and to establish a solid vision for your life.

7

This book will inspire people to believe in themselves and to understand that they can effect change in their life to the point where it will be impossible to return to the place where they once were. It offers methods and encouragement to empower yourself and to self-educate yourself towards new things. It turns people who are stuck in circumstances seemingly beyond their control into empowered, motivated "doers" who take charge of their lives and overcome adversity.

This book will open your eyes to the things that are within your control in your life, such as your effort, how you personally take things, what you believe, your priorities, what you think about, how open-minded you are, your happiness, and whom you surround yourself with.

Throughout this book, not only will I offer the mental strategies that have worked for me; I will also share my story with you: my hurts, happiness, successes, and failures—all as real-life examples. I will offer encouragement and tools to create a "can do" mentality and inspire you to get out of the rut you are in, move yourself forward, and become an inspiration to those around you, someone who has something to say and give back to others.

You will learn how to stand on your own two feet. You've heard the saying, "God helps those that help themselves." Another way to say it is, "The wind can't move a boat that doesn't have its sails up." Let's get those sails out, and let destiny take its course; let's help you help yourself.

After extracting myself from the dire situation with my father, I wound up in a serious relationship for several years. It proved to be very unhealthy, mainly because I did not know any differently yet. I had not yet developed my own sense of self-worth; therefore, I was ill-equipped to properly protect myself from someone who did not want me to succeed. I fell into the trap of allowing a victim-like mentality to settle in on me, and for years

I maintained a "poor pitiful me" attitude and even self-described a life that had bombed out on me. After five or six years of this defeat syndrome, I decided to permanently take responsibility for my own life—not only where it was but where it would go in the future. I left my abusive live-in boyfriend and sought out influences that would uplift and reinforce healthy behaviors, habits, and lifestyle. I sought counseling, read self-help books, joined church support groups, and surrounded myself with people who would be honest with me if I began to backslide. Today I am mentally healthy, happy, and successful—none of which would have been possible if I was not willing to be accountable for my own life and take things into my own hands. I had to want things to change and possess a desire to change myself and my mentality before it could happen. Then I had to fight for the life I wanted and deserved. I would like to ask you for three things as you begin this process with me. First, have an open mind. I promise you that you will not regret walking this path with me. We are going to walk through the forest into a beautiful clearing before long. Second, please make a commitment to yourself that you will do the hard work to improve your life. Third, use a journal while reading this book. In every chapter, I ask you to make specific journal entries that answer valuable questions. This will be used in several ways. It will be used for accountability and motivation, as well as later showing you how far you have come mentally and emotionally. It will ultimately serve as your roadmap for the future.

I have kept a journal for almost twenty years. I have used it to be openly honest with myself about what my thoughts and feelings are. I've also used it to chronicle what is going on in my life emotionally and spiritually, as well as to record my goals, successes and failures, and things I am learning. It's incredibly inspiring and motivating to read back on what was written and realize all that has happened and been accomplished over time. Anytime I feel like I'm failing and nothing has changed, I get out the books of my own words in ink, and I am completely overwhelmed at what has actually transpired in my life. My journals help me remember the things that have worked out, how my efforts have paid off, and all the blessings that have come to pass. They also help me realize that most of the things I have feared and worried about have never happened and that when I did stand still, it was as a result of being paralyzed by fear itself. My journals hold me accountable and have served as a tremendous motivator and tool for me in my self-help walk with continuous personal improvement. Journaling reinforces that while I have grown as a person, I am constantly evolving and I still have a long way to go. The journey will not end.

I look forward to trusting the journey ahead and sharing life's possibilities with you! With all that life has to offer, who knows WHAT'S POSSIBLE? Let's find out!

The secret of change is to focus all of your energy,
not on fighting the old, but building the new.
—*Socrates*

See things that are hopeless and yet be
determined to make them otherwise.
—F. Scott Fitzgerald.

CHAPTER 2

Stop Saying, "I Can't"...
Change Impossible to I'm Possible!

Why do you believe you aren't capable? What mistruths are you accepting as irreparable facts?

> **You must identify the source of the lies you have in your head and rip them off the interior walls of your mind, like old wallpaper that needs to come down.**

It might be easier to remain complacent where you are, but I assure you it is not worth it! You must develop a mental defense system that combats any negative thoughts you have about yourself and your abilities to change your situation. I know you are worth it, but in order to produce real change, *you* must believe that you are worth the effort to do so.

You are about to start a recovery process, a total identity system reboot. Stop sabotaging your own healing and eventual success with negative thoughts about yourself. Keep them from your mind. This will help you refrain from perpetuating negative things and cycles in your own life. Don't be your own worst enemy.

POSITVE = MORE

NEGATIVE = LESS

Clear your mind of "I can't."

Let's work on your first journal entry. Please make an honest list of all of your negative thoughts about yourself. Don't hold anything back. You know better than anyone where the smoke is in your negative thinking; let's find the fire so we can put it out!

Now, write the word "LIES" in capital letters across the top of the page. This exercise is about taking these lies out of your head and putting them on a page so you can purge them.

The first thing you need to realize is that there are things within your control that you need to get a grip on *right now*. Your thoughts are one of these things.

> **You are in control of your own thoughts.**

No one else is! How refreshing is this? In order to change impossible to "I'm possible," you must resist complacency and stop being a victim of your circumstances! It may not be your fault that you are in the situation you happen to find yourself in, but it is CERTAINLY your fault if you remain in an unhappy, unproductive state. If you realized how powerful your thoughts are, you would never think a negative thought again. Your thoughts are an incredibly powerful thing that you are in charge of, and you are up to the task of taking control of them.

During the thirteen years my parents were married, they made a series of about thirty moves. My dad was always chasing a new dream when someone (in his mind) did him wrong and made it impossible for him to succeed where he was. It was always better on the other side of the fence, and it was always someone else's fault that we did not have a better life. This mentality continued after he kidnapped us, so we were always on the road.

> **One can actually become warm and cozy while sitting in a big pile of cow manure!**

It's definitely warm, but it smells awful! Eventually it dries and becomes crusty and, instead of shaking it off for good, more fresh manure is heaped back on. Your circumstances may be like this, particularly if you've been in them for years. It may feel comfortable and easier to just remain and deal with the old familiar crap. You may be so ingrained in your way of life that you can't see a way out. You must convince yourself that you can change your situation. If you are uncomfortable with change, get ready! Complacency is a dangerous thing, and I want you to fight hard against it on a daily basis moving forward. It is a major road block to change.

You will first have to prepare yourself for the fact that change is imminent if you want your situation to improve. If you are serious about overcoming your circumstances, then change is inevitable. If you are stuck in a situation that seems impossible to solve, you will be able to extract yourself from the muck.

> **It doesn't have to get any worse than this at this moment in time.**

It is up to you if it does or does not. Deciding to clean the muck off your shoes is hard; don't fall into the trap of staying stuck just because it's seemingly easier to remain there.

A woman I was working with several years ago had a lot of potential but was really digging in and resisting doing the work to change her circumstances. She wanted something more out of life and had the ability to achieve what she dreamed of. I was challenging her to broaden her horizons and become more. She wanted the results; she just didn't want to put forth the effort that it would take at the time, nor was she excited about the amount of change she would actually have to undergo in order to rectify her circumstances.

She came to my office one day and told me she was resigning from her position with the company. I was caught completely off guard. When I asked her why, she offered this response: "I thought this weekend that it's just easier to not do this." It's just easier… the words set me off. I looked her in the face and told her bluntly that I was calling bullshit on her excuses and was not accepting her resignation. She could do this, and if she wanted to leave, she was going to have to walk out on me. She looked at me with tears in her eyes and committed herself to try harder. And she did. She pulled herself up by her bootstraps and took control. She went on to do some wonderful things for the company.

For you to move forward, it may be necessary to remove negative influences from your life. Sometimes these might be family, friends, coworkers, or even a job, in order to make room for your own dreams to flourish. Walking away from people, family in particular, is hard, and it's not always necessary. But identifying the unhealthy relationships that you have and their effect on your life is necessary in order to create change and make room for the things or people that will propel you forward. If you are going to eliminate "I can't" from your vocabulary and the negative voice in your head, you have to find a way to eliminate any unsupportive and unhealthy external factors.

> It is very important to realize that your value does not decrease based on someone's inability to see your worth.

As a teen, walking away from my father was the only option at the time. After the abduction and living as a fugitive for many years, he felt the need to control the outcome of my life in order to protect his own. He was the most important thing in the world to me, and I had to give him up in order to have any chance at a life of my own. My environment was incredibly controlled and abnormal, but I did not know anything different. We slept in campgrounds while on the road, sometimes in tents or at other times in the back of an old green Dodge van. Our food intake was controlled, and our dark brown hair had been bleached blond in order to change our appearance. We lived one whole summer in a campground in Arkansas while my brother had untreated pneumonia. We didn't even realize we were homeless.

I had to fight and etch out every little normal experience for myself. In the midst of all of this, I was always a dreamer. I read and daydreamed about what I would become, accomplish, and achieve once grown. As I became a teenager and started planning what I wanted to do as an adult, he sprang the ultimate surprise on me. He told me I would not be able to go to college because of his crime. We lived under assumed identities. In order to go to college, I would have to assume my real identity. I did not have a social security number because I was nine years old when he kidnapped us and my parents did not obtain our numbers before that. My and my brother's identities were flagged because we were FBI missing persons, and if either of us tried to get a social security number with our real birth records, the bureau would be notified. I would be found; therefore, my dad would be found.

Worse, I realized I was never going to be allowed to really leave the situation and have my own life. He had a vision for my future that I didn't even realize existed until I was about fifteen years old. At an age he thought appropriate for me, he planned on finding me a man to marry that met his approval, someone who would live with our family secret and live the life he wanted outside of normal society. I had no choice but to remove myself permanently from his life in order to have my own. I began planning and eventually executed my flight strategy at sixteen years old.

Once I made my decision, it was as though I had blinders on and could see nothing else in front of me except running as fast as I could away from the past and present and towards the future, *my* future, not his. It was as though God had a boot in the small of my back pushing me forward. There was no turning back for me, ever.

You cannot let someone else tell you what is right and wrong for your life. You must be the one to decide that.

Please take out your journal and write down every negative influence you feel you have in your life. Be honest with yourself, even if one of the negative influences is a person you love. Whether a person or a situation, list everything that is enabling your present circumstances. I want you to learn to rationally and logically identify things that are holding you back. Include thoughts on what others are telling you to do with your life. What decisions about your life are other people trying to impose on you? How does this make you feel?

Think of your life as a clear crystal glass. If it is filled with dirt, in order for you to fill it with fresh, clear water, you must first empty the dirt. That means that your glass will remain empty for a time until you begin refilling it. You may feel raw and empty for a while. This feeling is part of the process, and feeling empty feels dissatisfying. We naturally want to fill our holes. They make us feel awful. You'll need to replace all the dirt you've removed from your life's glass with more positive things that reinforce and support your journey. You can't begin to refill the glass with new dirt.

The very first thing you must replace is belief in yourself. If you don't believe in you, don't expect others to! Don't go back and pick up old negative influences or new ones disguised in a different package. Protect yourself from the old dirt, and keep the cow manure off your shoes. Spiritual reinforcement is incredibly helpful as well. You must be listening to the right voice as you move forward and get unstuck.

When I made the decision to run away from my father, I felt what I have always described as a "boot" in the small of my back getting me through it. Because of the circumstances, I felt as though I would be safer on the streets fending for myself than I was at home at the time. The final catalyst was a scene between me and my dad's wife. She asked me to go for a walk in the woods with her. She wanted to talk to me about my behavior. Sitting next to a stream, she absently looked around and said, "It's beautiful out here. It's so remote. Something could happen to a person, and their body would never be found." It was a veiled threat on my life, and I decided right then I was getting out. My mind was already gone; my body just had to catch up. I had few options regarding where I could safely go. A friend from school who was helping me to harbor my plan was willing to introduce me to some friends of hers in Austin that she thought would let me crash with them. I decided to call my aunt, my dad's sister, and to let her know that I was going to run away. Dad had trusted her the year before with our whereabouts, and this was the first contact with family we had had in the years since the abduction. I borrowed my brother's moped and rode it miles down country roads to a pay phone at a small store and placed a collect call to her. I told her my plans and that there was nothing that could change my mind. I was scared for my own safety. She asked me to give her two weeks and call her back. I did, and she and her husband agreed to take me into their home in Dallas. I had to get myself to her, but once I was there, she was willing to help me and protect me. I shared my plans with my little brother, who was fourteen at the time. I asked him to come with me. He did not want to. I offered to leave him enough money for a bus ticket to Dallas later. He refused. It crushed me to have to leave him there, but I did not feel that he was in the same kind of danger I was. He and I had been each other's only constant companions. To this day, we are the only other people in the world we have to talk to who actually know what it was like. A few weeks later, I concocted a story to allow for my absence from home, my friend drove me to the airport, and I boarded a plane with a small duffle bag and the clothes on my back. Once I got to where I was going, I crashed. I was consumed with guilt, shame, and fear of the unknown. I had just walked away from the only life I had ever known. Stinky as it may have been, it was what I knew, and it felt secure, in a sick kind of way.

When I called to tell my dad I wasn't coming back, he made every attempt through emotional manipulation to get me to come back and let him "help me" do this in a different manner. I stood firm and didn't step back into the pile of manure. I did not go back and pick up his burden and carry it. When his attempted emotional manipulation failed to get me to return, he turned into a raging, screaming animal full of violent threats against me if I did not meet his demands. Both my aunt and I felt that returning would put my life in more danger and that there was a real chance that he would kill me if he felt that was what he needed to do to protect himself from the things he felt threatened by. I will never forget my aunt's words to me: "If you give in and go back, they will kill you and dump your body in those woods, and no one will ever see you again." While I was terrified, it did not change the fact that I felt raw and alone, because my dad and I had been very enmeshed for so long. Day by day, my situation and feelings improved. With distance, I was able to begin the repair process. You can do the same.

Real change doesn't mean that you feel safe and secure. It can be painful, awkward, and scary, but that's how you know you're actually doing the work and truly shaking the foundations of the things that aren't working for your life anymore. Don't be afraid to dismantle and rebuild.

NOTES

Our goals can only be reached with a plan, in which we must fervently believe, and upon which we must vigorously act. There is no other route to success.

—Pablo Picasso

CHAPTER 3

Goals and Determination—Where Do You Want to Go?

If you've come this far in the book, you have no doubt decided that you aren't satisfied with where you are or the present state of circumstances that you find yourself in. You have faced the truth about your situation. You've decided you must make a move, but you may not really know where to begin the process. You must ask yourself, "Where do you want to go with this life of yours?"

> You only get one life; do you really want to spend it discontented and afraid to reach out for what you actually want?

The first mental step is to open the door to the future in your mind's eye and allow yourself to dream. No holds barred; don't start throwing up reasons why this dream isn't possible or that one isn't. You'll deal with barriers and strongholds later. Pretend there are no limits, and let your mind wander through the desires of your heart.

Allowing yourself to dream is such an important part of the process. It's a requirement for setting goals for your future, for the simple reason that it's easier to get there if you know where you are going. You've come this far and want to move forward. How do you step forward if the path isn't laid yet? To wander off down an unmarked path is dangerous and can lead to backsliding later on, but movement is the opposite of being stuck.

Believe me; I've been where you are now. For example, I allowed myself to get involved in an abusive relationship soon after leaving my dysfunctional family situation. You've got to begin to establish what the light at the end of the tunnel looks like. If or when you do veer off course, you'll have this dream and vision that is starting to form as motivation to get back on track and keep going.

We have established that in order to overcome your present circumstances and create the life you desire, you must allow yourself to dream. This will help produce vision in your life. Vision includes a bird's-eye view in your mind's eye of the past, the present and, most important to you, ... the future.

What did you dream of being and doing when you were a child? Before the mental, physical, emotional, and perhaps financial constraints were present that exist now, what were the things you would lie awake at night and dream of doing? What kinds of games did you play? Who did you pretend to be? What characters in books and movies did you admire? What teachers inspired you? Not only who did you want to be, but who did you NOT want to be? Who set negative examples of behavior and lifestyle that you wanted to avoid becoming? What cycles did you see others stuck in that you want to prevent or break in your own life?

Get your journal out and start writing down the answers to the questions I just asked you. Answering these questions will bring you back to a place where you were once free to make plans of going places. Dig deep and be honest with yourself. Your journal entry will help get things out into a tangible form, as you ponder these questions. As children we don't yet know the meaning of impossible; we have to learn what limits are.

> I challenge you try to return for a time to a state of "anything's possible."

My two-year-old grandson reminds me of this on a daily basis. There are so many things he wants to do on his own. He loves to be in the kitchen with me or anyone else, watching what is going on. He isn't tall enough to see that high, so he always wants "UP" onto the counter, to the highest level he can get—to see what is going on, what possibilities are up there for new things to do. He doesn't realize the danger of being up that high yet. He will learn that later. His desire right now is simply to rise above and see the big picture. He can't stand to be on the ground, looking up at things going on "up there" that he's not part of. Challenge yourself to dream of what's up there that you are missing out on.

Rise above, pull yourself up, and look around at the big picture of your life and the world around you.

> One of the most valuable lessons I've learned from my own life experiences is that there is always a bigger picture.

I can never see the entire thing, but my perspective broadens as I continue to mentally and emotionally rise above the place where I am now. I continuously feed my mind and soul so that the way I think is broadened, and the picture I see is therefore expanded.

Very often, things are not as they seem; therefore, learning that there is a bigger picture, even when you can't see it, will help you to establish a method to overcome barriers to getting unstuck. It creates a sense of faith and will strengthen your conviction that things are going to be okay.

Before running away from my dad, I began to rebel against the situation, hoping to change it. This scared my dad. He had to keep our family tight and controlled. We had a secret and a life of lies that had to be maintained. One little misstep from any of us would lead to our secret being exposed. He and my stepmother did their best to convince me that I was mentally unstable to be attempting to break free from the oppression and control I was under. I didn't conform; therefore, they had to shove me down. They literally convinced me that I was crazy and needed "fixing." I did not know how to play the game they were playing, much less win. I felt as if I was losing my sanity as I began to push back on what was going on in our family. I was scared of my dad for the first time in my life. I began to feel more and more disappointed in myself for wanting the things that I wanted, things that Dad said were wrong. I didn't understand why I wanted to wear stylish clothes and makeup when he said they were evil and bad things. I trusted him implicitly, and if he said it, then it must be true. After completing a weekend of punishment of pulling weeds with my bare hands on my knees in a pasture, I was defeated and degraded to the point that I believed that they were right; I was off my rocker and needed help.

On my own, I went to Dad and my stepmother and told them that I had thought long and hard about my behavior. I thought there was something wrong with me, and I asked them to please take me to a psychiatrist to get help. Dad was encouraged and somewhat proud of my realization. He saw there was hope for me to stay on the right track. His track.

On what was to be our last family counseling session intended to bring me to my senses, the counselor asked to speak to me alone. She said she wanted to ask me a few questions. They were: "Kim, what kind of grades do you make?" I made mostly As. "Kim, do you do drugs of any kind?" I had never tried any kind of drugs. "Kim, do you drink alcohol?" I did not use alcohol with friends. My dad believed that if I wanted to get drunk, I could do it at home, where it was safe, rather than being out somewhere. "Kim, do you smoke?" Never tried cigarettes. "Kim, are you sexually active?" Nope; I had never so much as made out with a boy, I was not allowed to go out with boys, and I was taught that premarital sex was a sin. "Kim, do you sneak out and do any of the things we just discussed?" No way. Our house, at the time, had bars on all the windows, so there was no way for me to sneak out, and I wouldn't dare anyway. "Kim, what are your hobbies?" I read a lot.

"OK, let me understand this," she replied. "You make excellent grades, you do not use drugs or alcohol, you have never smoked a cigarette, and you are not sexually active. You do not sneak around and go out. For fun, you like to read, and you spend most of your time with your family." Yes, that summed it up. She closed her notebook, laid down her pen, and looked at me with concerned eyes and said, "Kim, I have two boys and a girl, all teenagers. I want you to listen to me very carefully, because I don't think you will be coming back to see me. You are a good girl. You are exceptional, actually. I wish my own children walked the straight and narrow a tenth of what you are doing. You are a daughter any parent should be proud to have. I would be proud of you if you were my daughter. I'm not certain about what is going on in your family, but I am certain it is more than meets the eye. That's about all I can say to you, considering your age and this situation. I hope you understand what I am trying to tell you."

My heart rose in my throat, and I got butterflies. I was not crazy! This woman was sending me a message and trying to help me see there was more going on than I could see and understand. I knew I had to continue to rely on my instincts and believe in myself, no matter what the situation appeared to be or how it was being presented to me. There was a much bigger picture that I could not see from where I was standing.

When I am speaking to an audience, I illustrate this simple phenomenon by asking people to come stand next to me. I draw a circle around them, at the very limits of their vision. Then I ask them to stand on a box, and I redraw the circle to the limits of their vision again. That second circle is always bigger. Next, I pull the box back and once again draw a third circle to the limits of their vision. The third circle will be even broader. The point is that learning more and more empowers you to step back, step up, and think at new heights and levels than you did before.

Things simply are not always what they seem. I believed, at the time, that I was not kidnapped. I had gone with my dad voluntarily, and I had stayed until I did not want to stay any longer. That was how I saw things. Once reunited with my mother, I defended my dad to her over and over. We got into many arguments over it. I learned, over time and through counseling, that I had suffered from Stockholm syndrome, where victims feel responsible for protecting their perpetrators because they were their caregivers and only protectors during the time of captivity.

On my eighteenth birthday, I went to the Social Security Administration to finally get my social security number. It was an exciting day for me. When I walked out of that building in February of 1988, Kim Cook Williams Blake died, and Kim Casey emerged—for the first time since she was nine years old. Right after this, I set things in motion to be reunited with my mother.

We met in the parking lot of a school in the small town where she lived. It was incredibly emotional for both of us. She had no advance notice that I was coming or that I had not been with my dad for almost two years, nor did she even know if I was alive or not. We started trying to get to know each other and form a relationship. It was rocky in the beginning. For many years, I believed the things I was told by my dad about my mother. This served to harden my feelings towards her and made me want to fight for and defend what my dad had done; however, when I finally opened up and really allowed my mom to tell her side of the story, I realized that so many lies had been told to me. But I was not whole or mature enough to give my mother a real chance until many years later, when I was a woman in my midtwenties, influenced and inspired by my relationship with my small stepchildren. I was then able to begin relating to her as a woman, and we started and continued to bond more and more each year. As I became a woman myself and saw her hurts, it enabled me to think for myself and tear down the lies of the past in order to open the door for a special relationship with her. In my relationship with my mother, beauty was truly brought from the ashes over time.

Come to grips and be real with yourself about the place where you are now. Don't make excuses for yourself, and don't blame others. Take responsibility for the situation so that you are empowered to change it. Leaving things in the hands of others will slow things down or even halt your progress. Own the situation. If you do this, you become the force that creates the forward motion. Don't play the pity card on yourself, and don't say, "It's too late now." As long as you are alive, it's never too late to start afresh.

I will say this over and over to you: ***Things don't have to get any worse than they are today.*** Now that you have an awareness of the cause of your unhappiness, don't let your life continue to erode.

> Today can be your rock bottom, and, tomorrow you can begin climbing the ladder out of your pit.

It's up to you. If you really want something, you will find a way; if not, you will find an excuse as to why it isn't possible.

As you allow yourself to envision the life you want now, start to hone in and get specific about what you really want to accomplish. Please write these thoughts and visions down in your journal.

An abundant life starts with a picture in your mind of what you would like to do or be.

You may experience pain and even remorse as you open your mind to allow yourself to dream of a life other than what you currently have. That's okay; allow yourself those feelings, but keep pressing forward and think about what needs to change. Don't allow remorse to drown you and become yet another stumbling block to your future. Successful people don't have the lives they do without first going through a season of becoming. You have been becoming.

> *Regret that leads to change is a dear friend.*
> *Regret that leads to shame is an enemy.*
> —*Patsy Clairmont*

Letting go of an unhappy yet perhaps comfortable situation is not easy. Feel your feelings, but don't let them control you. Your new compass and guiding light are the vision and goals you are starting to set for yourself.

Professional athletes practice a concept in which they meditate and see themselves achieving the success they want. They envision, in their mind's eye, making the touchdown, skiing the slope, or making the goal. You can use the same technique to teach yourself to envision overcoming your circumstances or accomplishing new goals. Begin to see yourself there. Do it enough that you begin to get comfortable with the possibility of it becoming a reality. If you dream about it enough and achieve it in your mind, then when you physically get there, you won't be surprised, and it will feel like a technicality. The hard work is in your head.

I was not athletic as a young person. I had asthma my whole life, and exercise aggravated it. When I was in my late thirties, I decided to start running for exercise. For my thirty-seventh birthday, my husband bought me Nike Plus shoes to work with my iPod. It motivated me to do what I saw otherwise as incredibly hard. I could only run half a mile when I started. But the Nike Plus tool had motivational speakers who would give a pep talk any time the runners beat their own personal best in distance or speed. If I outperformed what I'd done previously, a world-class or Olympic athlete would come on and give me an inspiring speech. The speeches motivated me, but if I didn't do better, then I didn't get the talk. I needed to beat myself in order to obtain what motivated me. Once I figured this out, I used it as a tool to feed myself and push myself further each time.

A half a mile became one mile, then three. Eventually, I was able to run five miles. I remember jumping for joy in my yard when I ran five miles the first time and got an inspiring congratulatory speech from Lance Armstrong. As I progressed, I found myself believing I could do even more and considered running an actual road race. I ran a 10k, then a 15k, then a half marathon! The asthma attacks stopped, and I no longer needed medicine for the first time in years. The next normal step in my thought process was to consider the possibility that I could actually run a full marathon of 26.2 miles. I kept running, envisioning completing one more mile each time.

After a trip with some of my girlfriends to New York, I started dreaming of running the New York City Marathon, the world's largest race, which allows runners to see all five boroughs of the city on foot and finishes dramatically in Central Park. I knew I needed to stay motivated to achieve this new dream. I decided not only to run the marathon but also to make it even more significant and something I could not back out on. I signed up to run for a charity that honored one fallen NYFD fireman from the World Trade Center attacks. The charity provided scholarships for underprivileged high school students who had overcome tremendous adversity and gone on to achieve something in their lives. I spent hours running and envisioning myself crossing the finish line.

One day, I had a pain in my foot. A doctor examined me and said that I had a hairline fracture, put me in a boot, and said I was not going be able to finish my training in order to make the race. I was devastated and didn't want to accept it. So I got a second opinion. Thank goodness I was determined and would not take "no" for an answer! The second opinion found that I did not have a broken bone but a pulled tendon. With physical therapy and the right treatment, I would barely be able to finish training and make the race. On a cold Sunday in November, that vision turned to reality when I completed the New York City Marathon to celebrate turning forty years old. In addition to that, I was able to contribute almost ten thousand dollars to the scholarship fund for youth who were in places like those where I had once been.

For me, training for and finishing that race embodied the life I had overcome and the process I used to do so, as well as what I've accomplished since overcoming the adversity I originally inherited. It takes a disciplined approach to be truly successful.

Creating vision requires that you seek and obtain clarity over the past, present, and future. Obtaining clarity is a step towards motivation to move forward. How did you get where you are now? What is in your family history that perhaps led to the culmination of these circumstances in your life?

You need to come to terms with these things and identify what led to your situation. Where did this landslide start? You need to identify what the turning point or trigger was. It is critical that you understand and know these answers so you won't wind up there again, allowing history to repeat itself, manifested in a different set of poor circumstances.

Through my own personal discovery, there are many things I learned about both of my parents that helped me to understand them and, as an adult, to forgive them and myself. A big part of my healing was digging into their lives and pasts, then stepping back and taking a look at the big picture. The older I got, the more I could put myself in their places and understand them, therefore making it easier for me to forgive them.

My dad was raised by an alcoholic father who was very verbally and physically abusive to him. A victim-like mentality set in at an early age, and he was never able to shake it. He always seemed to feel as if the world owed him something. It was a generational bondage of sorts and a cycle that had to be broken. The more I learned, the more determined I became that I would do everything in my power to be the one to break this cycle so that it did not imprison me as it had him.

The last time my dad saw his father alive, I was ten years old. We had circled back through Texas on our journey. We lived in a small town, in a house with no furniture. We slept on the floor on foam mats and ate off cardboard boxes while sitting in the living room. My grandfather was smoking in the house and asked my dad if the smoke was bothering him. My dad said, "Yes, a little bit." To this my grandad replied, "I don't give a shit if it bothers you or not, you little bastard." Grandad left a day or so later, leaving our trashcan full of cigarette butts and empty whiskey bottles. I can remember watching tears roll down my dad's face as he told his father good-bye.

It hit me that he was probably saying good-bye for the last time. There was not one single "I love you" exchanged. There was only a feeling of hurt and regret at not being able to overcome the sickness so obviously ingrained in him that had caused so much pain. This was a glimpse for me into the hurt child that he was. It was also the first time I can recall having feelings where I wanted to fix someone else's feelings. I learned many years later it was the beginning of codependency issues for me.

Since I had confusing memories of my mother and my father's lies emblazoned in my mind concerning her, learning about her childhood and her marriage to my dad was so helpful in developing our relationship after we had been separated for so many years. I came to respect my mother incredibly and developed an amazement at all she had come through. It took an incredibly strong woman to withstand the loss that she did. I was nine and my brother was six when we disappeared. She lived for years, utilizing every law enforcement resource available to her in an attempt to recover us. Not only was she unsuccessful in this fight; she also went years not even knowing if we were alive until I showed back up in her life at the age of eighteen. My brother was not reunited with her until he was a six-feet-two-inches-tall twenty-seven-year-old man. It had been twenty one years since she had seen her baby boy. I have learned over time and have come to appreciate that I inherited my strength and ability to fight for myself from her.

I believe history repeats itself and so do dysfunctions within families. It is up to some people to try to look back, then to look at the big picture, and to break the cycle for themselves. My desire for my life has merely been to be able to look at myself and my circumstances, to rise above them, and not to be a victim. I don't want what happened to me or to my family to have such an effect on my life that I am miserable as an adult and can't even figure out why. I don't want to use my childhood as an excuse for not having it together as an adult. I have worked hard to develop an ability to look deep inside myself and recognize why I feel the way I do. Obtaining clarity over the situation has been incredibly important to me over the course of my life. Understanding the "why" behind my situation has given me some sense of power over what otherwise would feel like an out-of-control roller-coaster ride.

Spend some significant time writing in your journal and pondering a bird's-eye view of your circumstances. This is a deep exercise, but it's worth the effort to dig up and uncover the root of the issue.

After I ran away from my father and escaped the fugitive situation he had us in, I wound up being taken in by my aunt in Dallas. I spent over a year attempting to get my head on straight and figuring out what I wanted to do. I made goals and plans, and I dreamed of all that I could be, do, and become without the yoke of oppression and control around my neck. I did not, however, spend very much time considering what circumstances in my family's history had led up to the abduction. I did not yet seek to clarify the truth. I chalked everything up to what I had heard my dad tell me about the past, my mother, and the rest of my family. I swept it all under the rug and thought that I was moving on. Therefore, I was not equipped to defend myself in my new world. I was very vulnerable and, actually, a sitting duck. Sweeping difficult situations under the rug and ignoring them is not the same as truly moving beyond them. This behavior can do nothing but enable you to climb out of one pile of manure and step into a new one.

As I mentioned, near my eighteenth birthday I sought out my mother and let her finally know that I was no longer being held in captivity. She had not seen me or spoken to me since I was nine years old in 1979, when she said good-bye to me for what she thought was a normal visitation weekend with my dad. I was unsure of my feelings, having been through so much and believing the lies that I did, but we started the process of getting to know each other. Within a few months, it was decided that things were going well enough that I would move in with her and her husband. I made the move from Dallas to a tiny East Texas town where she and my dad had grown up. All of my relatives still lived there.

Although I was initially reunited with my mother, I still protected my dad. I refused to tell my mother about any of the places we had been. I did not know if I could trust her to not try to pick up the trail and continue the search for him to have him arrested. Even though I did not want to remain entrapped in his life, in my mixed-up mind, I somehow still felt obligated to protect his whereabouts. I asked my mother to contact the FBI and report that I was with her and no longer missing. My dad had picked up and run again, once I left, and as far as I knew, my brother was actually still with him. Once she did this, it was picked up by the media, and the news stations began to call. Several Dallas stations wanted to do interviews with us both. I refused to do so. I still didn't understand the truth of what had really happened, and all I was interested in was moving on with my newfound free life. I wanted to be a normal teenager and do the normal things that involved.

I had never had a boyfriend and had never dated. Dad had total control over our lives and who we associated with in order to protect the secret the family was harboring.

I got a job at the local grocery store, and there I met a guy whom I became seriously involved with almost immediately. It was a huge mistake and had long-lasting repercussions on my life. I simply was not equipped yet with the tools and emotional ability to be in a relationship. It wasn't evident to me at the time, because I thought I was in love, but I had just extracted myself from one extremely controlling situation and had the world at my feet. And instead of pursuing health and freedom, I jumped straight from the frying pan into the fire.

All the while, I began taking GED prep courses at the local high school to make sure I was ready for the exam. I had set a goal to earn my GED on what would have been my graduation date. I didn't want to be behind other people my age. The instructor pulled me aside after a few classes and told me that I didn't need these courses, that I was more than ready to take the test. I registered for the test in May of 1988, which was the month when I would have been graduating from high school anyway. I received my high school diploma in the mail and felt as if I had not lost one bit of time. I was on cloud nine.

My mother, whom I called by her first name at this point, helped me go through the financial aid application process and get enough grants to go to college. I had started school, I had a job and a boyfriend, and I was loving life. I felt like I had a normal life for a person my age, and that had been the goal I had set for myself. In my mind, I had overcome and achieved what I had set out to do, and there was nothing further that I needed to work on.

I didn't spend enough time with my new family, nor did I yet understand the importance of it. I wouldn't begin to understand this until later, when I met my future husband and stepchildren. I jumped right into the first relationship that came my way. Within a few months, I moved out of my mother's home and in with Ben. I was only eighteen years old, and my only previous relationship with a man had been the controlling relationship I had with my father. I had not learned what my triggers were and what situations I needed to avoid. I had only had a few months of professional counseling about what had happened to me.

Unbeknownst to me at the time, I re-created my structure and my relationship while living with my dad by living with Ben and allowing the relationship to take the turn that it did.

I became so absorbed in my relationship with him that I almost completely stopped seeing my mother. She and her husband had bought me a car, and it left a bitter taste in her mouth to keep making the payments when I was spending no time with her. She wanted it back. I was furious with her. Her demand that I return the car within two weeks left me in a real bind for transportation. I had no money saved, since I was a student and worked only part-time. This made me even angrier at her. In my mind, she had never had to do anything for me my entire life, nor had she had to bear the expense of raising me. I thought she owed this to me and was coming out cheap, and I did not understand how she could take away the one thing I needed that she was actually capable of giving me. This was an utterly complete bullshit mentality on my part, but I wasn't yet able to see the full picture, nor was I willing to accept responsibility for my own circumstances.

Not only did I have no money to buy a car, but I also did not have any credit. Since I had just got my Social Security number earlier in the year, when I emerged from hiding, I had the Social Security number of a one-year-old. I didn't see any choice but to drop out of college and get a full-time job.

Ben had begun nagging me about college, anyway.

"I don't know why you are going to college," he would say. "You are just going to wind up checking groceries for the rest of your life, so college is a waste of time."

He was starting to disapprove of me trying to get an education, and that was making me afraid I would lose him. I needed his approval and needed to please him.

I had straight As in my college courses, and I walked out one day and never returned. My grades were mailed to me at the end of the first semester, showing all Fs and a GPA of .9. I didn't officially let the school know I was dropping out; I just walked away, so all those Fs were recorded on my transcript. I figured this ruined my chances of ever getting back into college. This, along with other stupid decisions I made, started a snowball of years' worth of constantly digging out of holes in order to get back to square one.

"It doesn't matter," Ben said. "You'll just wind up fat and pregnant, working in a gas station anyway. College gets people nowhere."

While deep inside I didn't really believe this, I went along with it and tried to convince myself in order to please him. I had left my dad over this very subject, and now I allowed my boyfriend to keep me from my education. It's really unbelievable when I think back on it.

Kudos to Ben, because he was partially right about one thing. College in and of itself will not get you to great heights; however, education combined with initiative, hard work, determination, faith in something bigger, and belief in yourself will take you great places. Since deprogramming the negative thought patterns that I had once been infused with, I now have a very successful career in business, own a beautiful home, take spectacular trips with my loving husband, and have more than what I need in life. None of this would have been possible had I allowed my thoughts to remain in a pit of despair or had I continued to harbor a "less than" mentality.

I went to work full-time at a movie rental store to pay my bills and to pay for the used car I had to buy from the only lot I could find that would finance it for me. I blamed everything on my mother. In my mind, it was her fault I had to drop out of school and get a full-time job so that I could afford a car. I acted like a complete victim and continued to accept none of the responsibility for my circumstances. I was also lying to myself and everyone else. My mother taking the car from me gave me an excuse to succumb to the pressure of my boyfriend and to drop out of college. It was just easier than doing the work necessary to have a better life with all the things I wanted in it.

> You either get bitter and give in, or you fight and you get better. It is that simple. You either take what has been dealt to you and allow it to make you a better person, or you allow it to tear you down. The choice is yours. You decide.

I recently came across an old letter I wrote when I was about nineteen years old, during the time I lived with Ben. One of the sentences said, "Life has bombed out on me." I don't even recognize the person who wrote those words so many years ago. She is like an alien to me. I am now mentally unable to imagine that I ever wrote that, because I am now, in no way, even capable of thinking this way. Because of the work I've done, it is impossible for me to return to that victim-like mentality or that controlled and oppressed lifestyle. You, too, can change the way you think about your life and existing circumstances by learning about yourself and committing to learning new things to expand your mind and the way you see things.

At the time, before I started doing the necessary work, I slipped right back into a set of circumstances where I allowed my life to be completely under someone else's control, someone who did not have my best interests at heart. I simply was not armed with the tools and emotional intelligence to combat the situation. I had come to the middle of my own River Jordan and turned around and walked back to the side of the river I had started on, a place of captivity where I was comfortable, because that was the easiest thing to do and I could not see the bigger picture.

This was just the beginning. My relationship with Ben became physically and verbally abusive as time went on, and all of my time and activities became controlled by him, right down to the clothes that I wore. I didn't wear shorts or a swimsuit for years.

I did not have clarity over the past and the present; therefore, I was warm and cozy, again, in a new pile of manure that looked a little different—all the while lying to myself.

Remembering past dreams and coming to grips with how you want the present to change are necessary steps, but the visionary process doesn't stop there. You have to define where you see yourself in the future. Is it a new job or career change, finishing your education, living in a new town, exiting an unhealthy relationship, overcoming financial insecurity, overcoming emotional insecurity, or doing more with what you have?

Define what you want to accomplish. Your journal exercises are key here and will help tremendously.

Ponder these questions when developing your vision to move forward: Does your vision provide a powerful picture of what you and your life will look like in three to five years? Does it represent a dream that is beyond what you think is possible for yourself right now? Does it clarify the direction in which you need to move? Does it clarify what your focus should be? Does it clarify the position you should try to place yourself in? Does it clarify the activities you should pursue? Does it clarify the capabilities you need to develop? Does it give you a larger sense of purpose? Is it positioned in such a way that you see yourself building a skyscraper rather than sweeping the floor? Does it create a vivid image in your mind that provokes emotion and excitement? Does it give you butterflies in the pit of your stomach? Does it create enthusiasm and pose a challenge that inspires and engages you? Does it overcome any incapacitating thoughts you may have of yourself? Does your vision build on your own core competencies? Does it build on your own special history, strengths, unique capabilities, and assets?

Stop now and write these questions and the answers in your journal.

Not only must you find the confidence in yourself to fulfill your destiny, but you also need to develop a raging passion and determination to succeed. Without being selfish, ask yourself the question: How successful would I be if I worked as hard on my own dreams right now as I do to satisfy other people? This is one of the most important questions you can ask yourself. If you took the time to soul-search earlier in the chapter, you know what dreams lie in your heart, what talents you have, and where your strengths lie.

You absolutely must light your own fire.

> Ambition is the fuel that can drive life-changing events. Self-motivation is the force that keeps pushing you forward towards your vision and goals.

Wanting to do something and actually motivating yourself to do it are very different things. Motivation means action! It's the difference between whether you are capable of doing something or you are actually doing it. You absolutely must find what motivates you to move forward on this journey of continuous improvement in life.

You can absolutely be inspired by the words and actions of others, but the thing inside that drives you must be all *you*. You must find the boot in your back to self-propel. Establishing your goals and vision that we discussed earlier in this chapter will help you determine where your passion lies, as well as eliminating potential roadblocks to pursuing bold challenges and ambitious goals. You are already empowered to motivate yourself; you just need to accept the responsibility and hold yourself accountable. Self-motivation is the difference between those who accomplish their goals and those that don't. It's the glue that holds everything together. People who self-motivate don't let things get in their way or slow down their progress for long.

At one of the high points in my career thus far, I was the chief financial officer for a large corporation. I absolutely loved what I was doing, and I had driven myself to do some things I was proud of within the company over the years; however, at one particular point in time, my hands became somewhat tied to continue to make what I saw as positive changes with the company. Making positive change is what drove me. It had always come easy for me to find low-hanging fruit and accomplish something fresh and new on a frequent basis. Because of the constraints I experienced, I lost my motivation for a time, sat back, and became complacent and frustrated. The owner and CEO came to see me one day and discussed the change he saw in me. He told me, "Kim, you've been sweeping the floor, not building the building. You're a builder; get back at it." It was true. I had to circle back to what I knew worked and to relight my own fire and get moving. I had to work harder to get results.

Your journal is a must in the journey of continuous personal improvement. To motivate yourself, write down what you want to do and why you want to do it. Why are you motivated to achieve this in your life? This will keep you in touch with your true feelings on the matter and keep you focused on the driving force behind your goals. It will also help you see your progress, which is a huge motivating factor to do more.

> **Accomplishment is a tremendous stimulant.**

Allow yourself to think of former achievements in your life. Revive the feeling you had when you finished something you started or obtained a goal you had set for yourself. Remember the feeling you had and how it inspired you. You should almost be able to taste it. Now write about it in your journal.

Take a few more minutes and think about who you are as a person. Write down the answer in your journal.

You will need to latch onto your vision and what you want to accomplish and don't let go. Start to look towards the future. Once you realize you have it in you to accomplish what you dream of, remain focused on the next step towards that end. Looking to the future and not the past is a challenge for some.

> **The past is the force behind you, but looking to the future creates momentum in your mind, heart, and soul.**

Remember that time will pass anyway, so inspire yourself to be better tomorrow than you are today. It's a refreshing thought to think that with the right mentality, you will be a better person tomorrow than you are today, and better the next day than you are tomorrow.

You've spent some time looking back, analyzing what happened, and remembering some accomplishments.

> **We aren't going to dwell on the past in a remorseful way, however. It's a tool to be used to prevent history from repeating itself so we must pay homage to it.**

Dwelling on the past makes going back very easy, though. The past is important because it provides insight and clarity as to how we got where we are, but we absolutely must forgive ourselves and anyone else involved in creating our circumstances so that we can let the past go and move on. The goal is to break the cycle. You are effectively turning that which you once did not understand and held you captive into a tool you can use to wield power over your life.

At one point in my healing, I figured out that I had an overwhelming and unhealthy need to please my dad. I needed his approval of things that I did and of the person I was becoming in order to survive the circumstances at the time. I was fighting a losing battle. I was motivated by the need to make him proud of me. With help, I realized that not only was this never going to happen but also that it was actually a bottomless pit. I also realized that it was not a healthy driver for my behavior.

One of the first things I had to let go of was the need for my dad to be proud of me. It was incredibly painful to realize that no matter what I did, I would never have this. Can you imagine being a daddy's girl, yet one day realizing that your father doesn't like the young woman you are becoming? It was a devastating feeling, as though my entire world was coming to an end. As a teenager, and even into my early twenties, the reality would sometimes suffocate and choke me with emotion. The thought actually used to have enough power to bring me to my knees. I stopped letting the fact that I did not have my dad's approval steal my joy and control my direction. Once I was able to lay it down, to accept reality, and not try to change it, I made room for other healthy things to come in and motivate me.

The most courageous act is to think for yourself, ALOUD.
—Coco Channel

Be determined. If you are determined, you will be willing to do the hard work and heavy lifting.

To get to where you want to be in life, you will have to make some sacrifices. Determination and hard work breed sacrifice. The secret payoff? It's WORTH IT.

During the time I was training so hard for that first marathon, there was a lot of personal time I had to sacrifice in order to achieve my goal. There were many Friday and Saturday nights when I had to miss social events because I had to be up at the crack of dawn the next morning to run fifteen or twenty miles. I needed my mind and body to be rested and prepared. I always felt as though that training represented the process that I had used to accomplish some of my life goals. If you want something, you have to be willing to exchange something else in order to have it. This is basically bartering with yourself and determining what a priority is. What are you going to give in order to get what you dream about?

> I would rather be completely exhausted from the hard work and hard times that breed success than well-rested from achieving nothing.

Continuous effort, not strength and intelligence, is the key to unlocking potential.
—Winston Churchill.

Perseverance is to abide under the load. It is active, not passive. Difficulty is the only path to wisdom and growth. The longer you slumber, the longer you will remain in your poor circumstances. Laziness leads to poverty every time, whereas diligence and conviction lead to prosperity. You must develop and hold onto the conviction to press on toward your destiny.

You will need to commit to fan the flame in order to stay motivated. Play to your passion and find people who will support you and encourage you to keep going. You must become a self-fed, self-motivated person in order to make things happen for yourself. To grow yourself, you must plus your passion, feed it steroids. This is a test of creativity. Create avenues of thought and action that build your passionate desire to continuously improve your life.

Some examples of ways you can do this are as follows: putting yourself in positions where you are around people who are doing what you want to do, watching movies and reading books related to your dreams, and doing anything to keep what you are passionate about achieving in your line of vision and alive in your imagination. When things get out of sight, they get out of mind. You need to keep what you want in constant view so that you create a sense of constant desire. Understanding you are responsible for motivating yourself will help you when you are tempted to quit. You are in control of many things in this process.

Barriers to entry are those things that you feel are holding you back from accomplishing what you desire. They are strongholds that have to be overcome. They are mountains that must be moved.

Fearing failure and fear of making mistakes paralyze us and keep us from branching outside of what is comfortable and from picking ourselves up out of that warm, cozy pile of manure. There is little chance you will develop your potential if an overwhelming sense of fear is holding you back. Fear is the killer of dreams; however, if you are confident and free of those nagging fears, you will be able to develop your potential and succeed at what dreams lie in your heart. It is important to understand that we were not originally created with a spirit that makes us a slave to fear. Fear is learned behavior, not original behavior. Fear has tremendous power over us if we allow it to hinder our progress in life. Eliminate the fear of failure, and you will remove its power.

We had to learn to be afraid; we aren't intended to be afraid.

Don't be afraid to fail. Be afraid to not try.

> You gain strength, courage, and confidence by every experience in which you really stop to look fear in the face. Fear is a liar, plain and simple.

You may feel afraid because you feel undeserving of anything better than what you currently have.

You may feel like you don't deserve to achieve your big dreams. This type of fear hinders your ability to fulfill the purpose for which you were intended. Eliminating low self-esteem will change what you feel you deserve, which will, in turn, help you be less fearful. Enthusiasm must overshadow fear. My fear these days is not of trying and failing, but rather of NOT trying and being less than I might have been.

When I do get anxious and worry about an outcome, I remind myself that 99 percent of anything I've ever worried about has never happened. This is a real tool to combat my own mental stronghold of fear when it sets in, and it sets in often. No amount of worry can change the past; it is inconsistent, irrational, and ineffective. Worrying effectively carries tomorrow's load with today's strength. Carrying two days at once zaps your strength by moving into tomorrow ahead of time. It also does not empty tomorrow of any problems, but it does empty today of its strength and joy.

I am terribly and irrationally afraid of heights. I get nervous standing on a ladder three feet off the ground. A few summers ago, we took our son, our daughter, and her husband to Las Vegas for a vacation. Everyone wanted to do the zip line over Fremont Street. Even though I was scared, I paid for the ticket and committed to do it with the family. I got all the way to the top and was physically so anxious I could not get into the equipment. Everyone zipped without me, and I had to be embarrassingly escorted back down the tower. My son-in-law jokingly told me,

"One day, you are going to tell little Ellis [my grandson] that he can do anything he wants to do. I'm going to tell him to ask you about this day." It's true. To this day, I have regret about not facing my completely irrational fear. His statement, however, provided me with some inspiration and a vision in my mind of something that I never want to happen. I never want to be a hypocrite to my precious grandson or anyone else I try to inspire. I never want to stop practicing what I preach. It has become motivation for me to overcome this irrational fear of mine.

Spend some time in your journal recording things that you are afraid of. What triggers your fears? Get your arms around what is feeding this part of you. Understanding it and getting control of it will enable your enthusiasm to begin to overshadow your fears.

Not knowing yourself well may be something that is holding you back. Know yourself well, and turn your liabilities into assets. Understand your strengths and weaknesses. How well you will be able to deal with things in general is going to depend on how well you utilize the resources you have: all of your positive and negative qualities. Some obstacles can be considered resources, depending how you choose to make use of them in the course of your life.

As a human being, I'm sure you've been subject to circumstances that you've never expected to encounter. Perhaps you've had to take care of an older relative or to assist someone with a debilitating illness. While this can be a trying time for everyone, I expect you walked away with a degree of empathy or compassion you didn't realize you had. Or perhaps you've performed an act of charity by providing something so very basic to someone you have taken for granted and that "something" was entirely out of the person's reach. Did this not remind you of the simple lesson of gratitude for your own blessings that can sometimes be easy to overlook?

Perhaps you grew up in poverty and now have the capacity to understand what that means for someone still in that situation in a way that will help you impact change in that person's life.

Maybe there have been circumstances where you felt you did not rise to the occasion and could have chosen a different action. What did you learn then about what you can do differently in the future? All of our actions, our negatives and our positives, are blueprints to how we can propel ourselves upward and improve upon ourselves.

> Self-improvement is a never-ending journey, and we never stop learning. Strive to never stop learning.

Use your journal to list what you see as your weaknesses; then spend time listing your strengths.

Your own excuses are likely a wall you must scale as well. Look them in the eye and slay them. Here are some common mental excuses I often see and hear from people and have used myself:

1. "I don't have the time." To which I offer: we all have the same amount of time. How are you spending yours? Your time is your most valuable commodity. You can find some fragment of time to work on the most valuable asset you have, which is yourself. People find time to do what they really want to do.
2. A victim-like mentality. Life circumstances and personal traits can be seen as either positive or negative; it's up to you how you make use of the hand that life dealt you. Everyone's life is filled with a certain number of disadvantages, yet these so-called disadvantages can be turned into weapons used to win the race you have set out to run. Identify and bring your own personally advantageous qualities to light, and don't be

afraid to use them. Find a fresh perspective and explore your options. Don't be afraid to look at unconventional, perhaps even outrageous, methods to keep yourself moving forward. Don't wait for permission. Realize that nothing will get done if you don't take the lead and move into action. Free yourself to make decisions affecting your life rather than waiting for direction from others. Watch your ego; be confident and competent but humble.

3. Not willing to do the hard work. First of all, if you aren't in love with what you are trying to do, you will never work hard enough to be the best you can possibly be. It is absolutely amazing what you can do if you simply try. Don't dodge this bullet.

4. Procrastinating and simply not starting. I was inspired by a sign I once saw on a store front on a trip to Mexico. It read, "Somedays we are open, somedays we are not." The store happened to be open that day. It was "someday." How much time do we spend pining away for "someday" and our dream life and miss the fact that we just need to start? TODAY is someday. We are on a stage now; what are we going to do? Stop waiting to start living the life you want.

What are *your* excuses? What are your barriers to entry? Take some time and write about them in your journal.

If you see you are making an excuse for yourself, just face it and eliminate it. It's better to be honest with yourself and acknowledge your own laziness than continually make excuses not to do what you have set out to do. Do not take the easy way out by making excuse after excuse, and throwing up one imaginary wall after another.

You are being held in captivity, of sorts, that is preventing you from getting out of this rut and moving forward. Your captor may be a person, thoughts, or experiences. Either way, you are being lied to if what is holding you hostage is controlling you and holding you back. You and your thinking are all that actually restricts your growth.

At one point during our journey with my dad, he had a small music store in downtown Coos Bay, Oregon. We lived in the back of the store. During the day on the weekends, I curled up under the stairwell and read for hours on end. My little nook was on the other side of the wall to the back of the checkout area. Furnished with a foam mat, a lamp, and a cardboard box to hold my clothes, it served as my bedroom. I could easily hear conversations that my dad and stepmother thought were private. On one such day, I overheard them discussing pills. On another occasion, I saw a man come into the store and hand her a package wrapped in aluminum foil, and she reached under the counter and gave him some cash in exchange for the foil-wrapped package. Later that day, from my little cubbyhole, I heard Dad ask her, "Did you get the pills?" I assumed that they were using some kind of drugs. I became very angry. I could not understand why I was held to such a rigid set of rules and somehow it was okay for them to pop pills and pretend to me that they were perfect. It was the first time I noticed inconsistency in what was being demanded of me and what was practiced by them. A seed had been planted that started to grow. This was the beginning of my realization that the life we were being coerced to live was not real or right. I began to think it was built on lies.

Keep in mind that you may face opposition when you try to make positive changes in your circumstances and life. Those people who feel threatened by your transformation may try to dissuade you. Don't allow other people's opinions to mean more to you than your own positive opinion of yourself. Any people in your life that are holding you back are less than perfect themselves and quite possibly may be attempting to detract from their own issues by keeping you oppressed and downtrodden. It is often what drives oppressors and their treatment of you.

Use your strengths and confront your weaknesses to elevate yourself, and don't be afraid to dig deep. By knowing ourselves we strip away the power of outside sources to make us deviate from what we ultimately desire in our lives and future goals.

NOTES

Hold a picture of yourself long and steadily in your mind's eye and you will be drawn to it. Picture yourself vividly as defeated and that alone will make victory impossible. Picture yourself vividly as winning and that alone will contribute to immeasurable success.
— Norman Vincent Peale

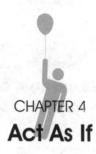

CHAPTER 4
Act As If

What does success look like to you?

It is so important to define this in writing in your journal because, as we've discussed, your vision will become your reality. Bringing it to fruition depends on you and your own attitude. Spend some time writing out your thoughts on this.

> Your definition of success will change over time—from accomplishing a specific goal to broader, bigger versions of accomplishment. It will become more fluid, like a moving river, and a way of life. It will guide you and begin to help you remain true to yourself.

Mine has evolved over time. My definition of success, straight from my own personal journal, now reads: To use what I have to create more by being productive and fruitful with the time, money, and talents that have been allotted to me. To inspire others to achieve more than they thought possible. I do not want anything to be wasted or in vain.

One of the challenges to dreaming big dreams is that often the first step is invisible. I'm going to ask you to focus on "acting as if" you are already there. Martin Luther King Jr. said, *"Faith is taking the first step even when you don't see the whole staircase."* Have faith in yourself and the mental possibilities you have created for your life.

Even though fear may make you believe to the contrary, you are not going to fall off a cliff by taking this first step; however, by standing still, you will eliminate the possibility of anything. That is quite simply too costly to you.

When we choose to believe in things not yet come to fruition, we tap into the power of what's possible, we overcome the status quo in our lives, and a limitless supply of options and potential outcomes opens up. Do you recall the mental strategy that was discussed in an earlier chapter that athletes use to envision success? That was a mental "act as if." Consider this chapter to be a physical "act as if." I will ask you to act as though you already have something you want or are the person you want to be. There is a big difference in envisioning something and dreaming it and actually living it. You've done the work to create your mission and vision, based on your own internal values and qualities. Now we will begin to physically bring those dreams to life and make them real.

"Act as if" boldly implies action on your part. I'm asking you to move beyond just thinking, dreaming, visioning, and writing in your journal. I'm asking you to act on what you've learned. Hold the picture of the dream you've created in your mind and begin to act as if it were already true. "Acting as if" means that you adopt the right mind-set for your own set of circumstances. It means acting as though you already have something that you want.

Let's begin with acting as if we are happy. Happiness is a choice, and all people can make that choice for themselves.

It has been scientifically documented that 40 percent of our happiness is within our control.

"Acting as if" starts with choosing to be happy. We can choose to be controlled by our circumstances and be miserable today, or we can choose to be happy today. If you are unhappy, then act as though you are happy. Our outsides reflect our insides, so put a smile on your face. Even if you don't feel happy, smiling has been proven to boost your mood. Actively look around, as you go through your day, for something that will make you smile. Find a child playing, a rainbow, a sunrise or sunset, an old memory. Find something to smile about today. Smiling when you are not happy makes you feel happy. It makes you want to do good things. How exciting it is to know that people can alter their lives by altering their attitudes!

In your journal, make a list of things you are grateful for. Gratitude leads to happiness. Go through the behavioral actions necessary to create happiness in yourself.

Happiness is like love; it is a verb, not a noun. Choose to act happy, and you will be happy. You must decide if you are going to choose happiness. Your happiness is in your own hands, no one else's. It is one more thing that is within your control. Stop letting people and circumstances steal your joy. You can be unhappy with your present situation, but choose to be happy with life in general and where you are headed.

People can't be happy if they are downtrodden and full of self-pity. Stop feeling sorry for yourself and be grateful for the chance you have to turn your life around.

You can't be happy if you are a victim of your circumstances.

> **Victims are a negative product of an imperfect situation.**

You are deciding to turn your imperfect situation around and produce something positive from your particular set of circumstances. No longer are you controlled by what has happened to you. You are choosing to use the lessons you learned to change your life. You are no longer the victim you once were. You are choosing happiness.

Take what is yours; just take it. This is not entitlement I speak of, but mentally and physically emulating the behaviors necessary for success in your vision. "Acting as if" involves seeing it, feeling it, doing it, and owning it.

Decide to own your vision and embrace it. It's yours now, and you can bring it to life. No one can take it away from you. You gave birth to this dream, you've documented it, and you will soon begin educating yourself as to what it will take to be the person you want to be and have the life you want to have.

Adopt the right mind-set for your own set of circumstances by gaining an understanding of what you need to get there. If your particular desire is about money and you want to be wealthy, then educate yourself regarding common traits among millionaires and start adopting them. This will help you get a better understanding of what you have to do in order to achieve wealth. Adopt the attitude a financially wealthy person would have before you actually become wealthy. In other words, if you want to be rich, then find out how rich people think and act, and start thinking and acting like a rich person. I don't mean spending all you have on foolish things and living outside your means. I mean learn what makes rich people tick and what drives them. What are their consistent behaviors, and how did they get to where they are?

This will help you handle your success when you achieve it rather than make mistakes and squander it.

My husband and I both came from very poor upbringings. When we married, we were both in debt and barely making it. He had just been through a divorce, and I had taken all the debt from my and my boyfriend's comingled finances, while he kept all the assets. I took home seven hundred dollars per month after taxes. While things got better every year because of our hard work, after five years of marriage, we were still deep in debt and nowhere close to where we wanted to be. We had dreams of being financially sound, but we knew nothing else to do except to work even harder. We decided to start putting ourselves in situations that were out of our financial league, so to speak.

We planned our fifth wedding anniversary celebration months in advance and saved enough for a fancy hotel and dinner. We got dressed up and drove to a five-star restaurant and hotel in Dallas. We pulled into the valet parking lot (something we never did) in his big Dodge pickup truck among all the BMWs and Mercedes. It was the nicest place we had ever experienced, and we were very uncomfortable. We felt like two kids from the country. We were embarrassed, didn't feel like we deserved to be there, and were certain that everyone was staring at us. Of course, all of this was bull crap concocted in our own minds. We drank opulent cocktails at the bar, ate an expensive meal in the restaurant, and stayed the night in a hotel room that cost several hundred dollars.

We continued to force ourselves to do things like this and eventually became more comfortable going to nice places like that. We eliminated the thoughts from our mind that those situations were out of our league or that we didn't deserve to be there. We put ourselves in that league. There were times when we could not afford to stay at such places. Those times we would simply go sit in the lobby bar among the people who were of the financial status that we wanted to be one day. It became more and more comfortable. My husband tells the story to this day and remembers how uncomfortable it felt. He uses it to inspire others to get outside of their comfort zone with regard to who they are and what they think they deserve. It was a pivotal practice that we adopted, and it changed the way we think. Education and broader horizons always change the way you think.

Over time, we also learned all we could about sound financial management and changing bad habits. Through my career path, I learned more and more about the mentality of wealthy people and realized that the way in which my husband and I saw and treated money was never going to get us where we dreamed of being. We changed how we acted before we ever actually had financial freedom so that our behavior and attitude matched the behavior and attitude of those who did have such freedom. We stopped living beyond our means, stopped buying things that were wants and not needs, and stopped buying things to fill a hole meant to be filled with things that aren't material. Over a few years, we saw an incredible impact. The behavioral changes, combined with the mental shift and our continued hard work, eventually led us into a situation where we did not have to struggle financially any longer.

Once in my career, I had an employee who had incredible potential. While she lacked formal education, I felt she had what it took to become a vice president someday. I told her she had to look, to act, and to walk as though she were the VP rather than a manager. That was the only chance she had of actually becoming the VP in reality. My theory was that if she took on the role, without being promoted, then she would get noticed as being that caliber of manager. She had been thinking the complete opposite—that someone would give her the chance, promote her, and then she would start assuming the role of a VP. I wanted her to turn her behavior on its end. I believe that you can be whoever you want to be, title or no title. Start acting the part and see where it leads.

Several years later, this particular woman was indeed was promoted to vice president. She was the second female to have been ever appointed to an executive-level position in the company.

If you are waiting on someone to serve your desires up on a platter, then stop right now and take responsibility. Take matters into your own hands. Don't wait for someone else.

Take some time in your journal to make a list of all the things you are waiting on someone else to do so that you can move forward towards the destination in your mind.

Become an owner of whatever you are doing.

> You are the sum total of your parts, your past, and your ambitions, and you get to determine your future.

It is never okay to settle for good enough when you can achieve remarkable. It's often all too easy to get caught up in the mundane aspects of our lives and our responsibilities. In the example of my former employee, she owned her tasks, and she excelled at them. She learned to not let anyone else's perceived view of her résumé temper her own expectations. Instead, she forged her own path by owning her goals, her strengths, and her drive to achieve. That behavior was noticed by others, and she was rewarded for it.

> Whatever you want to do and be, you have to start to play the part and get comfortable with the role.

If you do, you will gain confidence in yourself and what you have set out to achieve.

Eliminate the poverty syndrome; believe you deserve more. I refer to the poverty syndrome in more than a financial way. I have defined it as a "less than mentality."

> If you act as though you have nothing and deserve nothing, that is what you will always have.

You cannot think like this and achieve a life of abundance. "Acting as if" raises your self-esteem and provides the boot straps you need to pull yourself up out of this mind-set.

Another way to "act as if" is to dress for success. I have always asked my female employees to dress professionally. I don't expect suits every day, but I expect them to dress like the persons they want to be or the positions they want. If someone tells me they don't have the money to dress nice, then I help show them how it is possible. We eliminate that excuse right away. Dressing the part makes you think like the player. If you put on football pads and a uniform, you'll feel like a football player. Whatever the uniform, wear it.

When I first started my career, I practiced "dressing the part" daily. This was a result of a mentor I had early on. At that point in time, I did not have the money to buy expensive business clothes. Thanks to my poor upbringing, I was used to shopping in thrift stores. I found a Salvation Army store in Dallas closest to one of the highest-end residential areas of the city. I began frequenting the place weekly. The wealthy women from the area donated their clothing at this particular store, and I used this strategy to get my hands on things that were otherwise out of my reach.

I could find new things, or things with dry cleaning tags on them, that were incredibly nice and, quite often, high-end designer brands. I could buy designer business wear for six dollars per piece in that store. Essentially, I had a beautiful, classy wardrobe for less than what clothes cost at Walmart. When I got married, I knew I wanted a Jessica McClintock dress, but

I could not afford one. It cost almost four hundred dollars at a department store. For months, once a week, I looked at the Dallas Salvation Army thrift store and finally found what I wanted for twenty dollars. My point is that where there is a will, there is always a way. You just have to put the effort into getting creative and figuring it out.

Put yourself in situations your former circumstances or insecurities would not allow. It leads to building self-confidence and eventually comes naturally. More and more exposure often lays the brickwork on the path to your ultimate goals.

To sum things up, there are two necessary steps to "acting as if" in order to achieve anything big or small:

1. Hold a picture of the dream in your mind.
2. Act as if it were already so.

Take a few minutes to answer these questions in your journal: Who is doing what you want to do? Why are they successful?

To be a great champion, you must believe you are the best. If you aren't the best, then pretend you are.
—Muhammad Ali

NOTES

A mentor is a brain to pick, an ear to listen,
and a push in the right direction.
—John C. Crosby

CHAPTER 5

Pick a Mentor

It's often said that we are the approximation of the five people we spend the most time with. The people we surround ourselves with either raise or lower our standards. They help us to become the best or worst versions of ourselves. Because of this, we all need people in our lives who raise our standards, remind us of our potential, and challenge us to be the best we can be.

Who is doing what you want to do? Who is living your vision?

Books, speakers, and the other motivational tools you have in your kit are powerful items that you cannot do without on your journey as a self-motivated lifelong learner. However, they alone will not be enough to provide 100 percent of the strength you need to change your life circumstances. You need to choose a mentor to be most effective and to enhance your growth.

Nothing can replace the empathy and advice of someone who has powered through challenges, overcome adversity, and accomplished what you are seeking to do and who also cares about seeing you succeed. Having access to someone who has "been there and done that" and who is willing to use his or her story to help you get where you want to go is incredible. The guidance of a wise and trusted mentor can give supersonic speed to your efforts to overcome the factors that have been holding you back.

> Some of the longest-lasting lessons in my life have come from the shortest conversations with mentors.

Sometimes we need to hear aloud from someone else the thing we are most afraid to speak of or dare to dream about. The most meaningful conversations with mentors flipped a switch in me and caused me to go into high gear. Once your eyes are opened to the truth of your behavior or a situation, it is impossible not to act on it unless you are plain lazy or simply just don't care. Neither one of those things is the case if you have come this far in this book.

Prepare yourself internally and make room for mentorship in your life in order to to be successful. This is a very important step. If you are not ready for mentorship, you will become frustrated, and the persons you have sought out as mentors will feel like they are wasting their time. You don't want to burn bridges with persons who could prove to be invaluable in your journey forward by not being ready to accept them into your life. To prepare for this part of your transformation, you can follow specific steps to get ready.

First, be acutely aware of your own particular weaknesses and vulnerabilities based on your past experiences and set of circumstances. Identify them and write them in your journal. Compare them to what you have written previously in your journal regarding your weaknesses. Becoming intimately familiar with your own triggers and the points where you've gone wrong in the past will give you the knowledge necessary to communicate them to your mentors, giving them the opportunity to have your back when you are tempted to veer off course.

Years ago, I became a friend and mentor to a young woman who is many years younger than me. While our relationship has changed as she has grown personally and professionally, we still enjoy a very close and special relationship today. She has identified her own greatest weaknesses and let me know what they are. In her mind, this gives me the opportunity to have her back and call her out when I see those weaknesses creating problems in her life. This young lady, in particular, has a problem with anxiety and worry. This sometimes holds her back from getting out of her box. I am usually able to put things in perspective for her and help her see that she is making things bigger in her mind than they really are, which in turn leads to a step in the right direction for her.

Second, your mentor must have similar values to yours. For you to identify if that is the case, you will need to know your own personal values, where you stand on things, and what you feel strongly about.

We have talked a lot about your own mission and vision. Just as important are your own personal values. Just as a business must define the culture it seeks to create by defining its mission, vision, and values, so must you define these things in writing personally. Creating your mission and dreaming of your vision are only the first two steps. Without values, you will not be able to successfully bring your mission and vision into reality. They are your guiding light and beacon to help you maneuver through the forest.

Use your journal to write down your own values. These are nonnegotiable terms in your life.

Some of my values are:

- Do the right thing, even when it appears doing so will have negative consequences for me.

- Remain true to myself; do not be swayed by other people's issues.
- Stand up for what I believe in.
- Be a good steward.
- Never get complacent and stop learning new things.
- Be an inspiration to those around me.
- Do not take advantage of other people's weaknesses.

The third step in preparing yourself for being mentored is to lay down any insecurity or embarrassment regarding where your life is today. If you are ashamed and scared to share what has happened to you, you will never be able to open up to a potential mentor, nor will you be able to move on to the next step in this journey and pay what you have learned forward. For many years, guilt and shame hung over me for backsliding. It was impossible for me to move forward during those years. Progress came when I was honest with myself and others about where I was and I stopped being ashamed of it. You must get over the hump of personal embarrassment and be honest with whoever you identify that would like to mentor you. You must trust your mentor. Real trust at this level is not the same kind of trust as if I trust you or you trust me with your bank account. Trust at this level means that you have found someone you can expose your inner self to and that such a person will not take advantage of your vulnerabilities. In short, this is vulnerability-based trust, and unease with this idea is just another fear distractor.

Take a moment to make an honest list in your journal of everything you are insecure about, ashamed of, or embarrassed of. Don't lie to yourself; get it all down. You will want to find someone you can trust with the information. You also have to be willing to let the past go in order to move on.

Letting go means you no longer allow your feelings to control your behavior or negatively impact your present or future.

When setting out to choose a mentor, it is important to identify someone with qualities that will enable a successful and meaningful relationship. If all goes well, this relationship will last for years to come. A true mentor commits for an indefinite period of time.

You may want to consider, as mentors, people who have experienced and overcome challenging circumstances themselves to get where they are. If your potential mentors have been through some challenging times and have overcome their circumstances in order to accomplish their success, then they will be well-suited to offer sound advice as you move through the obstacles you have set to overcome yourself. They will also have empathy for your circumstances and be able to offer hope and encouragement that what you are attempting to do is indeed possible. They will also know that what you are trying to achieve is actually possible based on their own personal experiences.

Your mentor must be a dedicated lifelong learner. This is an absolute must. You want a mentor that will encourage and promote constant growth through self-empowered learning. This is critical because you don't want to surround yourself with someone who believes that once you accomplish one set of goals, you are done and have arrived at a plateau where it is safe to become complacent and in a rut. That's a similar but different, although higher, location than you just committed to move away from. You want a mentor who will encourage you to never settle and to always commit to learning more so that you can dream more and therefore do more. This journey of yours is a fluid situation, and you will never arrive at a place where it is okay to just stop.

You and your mentor must be aligned in your basic principles and beliefs. If you are not, then you may expose yourself to the advice of someone who actually is of little help at all. Worse, that person could be damaging to your walk forward. You want to associate yourself with people stronger, even more convinced than yourself, who can help you build your spiritual, mental, and emotional muscles beyond where they are now. You are trying to develop into the best possible version of yourself. Choosing someone who is not aligned with your own values can also expose you to someone who may take advantage of your situation. I have been incredibly fortunate to have had more people take me under their wing than I had take advantage of me.

Develop an understanding of what your expectations should be of good mentors and how to work with them. You need to prepare yourself for what it will be like in order to minimize hurt feelings on your part if they critique your current way of operating or behavior. A "yes person" would only serve to allow you to continue the behaviors you are looking to outgrow.

Good mentors will challenge you and not accept your excuses. Your mentors are there to help you move forward and overcome the obstacles you have allowed to infiltrate your life. They are not there to baby you or to enable you to keep doing the same things you have always done. Don't expect them to validate your unhealthy or dysfunctional lifestyle or habits. While that might make you feel good temporarily, in reality it actually hurts you. You do not want mentors who will enable you to remain in that stinky pile of manure. If they do, they are not the right mentors for you. The right mentors for you will have the courage to stand up to you and your excuses, even if they fall out of favor with you as a result.

One of the first and most valuable mentors I had was an extremely beautiful and successful businesswoman who was my boss when I was twenty years old. She was extremely tough on me. As a matter of fact, at the time, I did not think she was very nice to me at all. I confronted her about it once and accused her of being unfair and harder on me than anyone else who worked for her. As I sat across from her desk, she pointed one bright red, polished, and perfectly manicured forefinger at me and firmly said, "That's because I want you to be all you can be." She didn't coddle me, and she didn't try to deny anything; she just told the truth. She had a huge impact in my life, but it was in hindsight that I saw it.

In my next job, I overheard my bosses one day saying, "It is so nice to finally have someone around here who knows how to actually do this stuff." As a huge smile spread across my face, I realized that that "stuff" was the very things I had previously whined at my former boss about being too tough on me.

Expect your mentors to hold you accountable and to be honest with you, even when it hurts. They will want the best for you, and they will feel successful when you are successful. Sincere mentors will be very motivated by your success, because it means they are being effective. In the same way that parents want their children to have better lives than they had, the best mentors feel a tremendous sense of reward when those they are mentoring exceed what they have actually done themselves. They won't want to hold you back. If they are successful as mentors, over time you could surpass their accomplishments, and they will not feel threatened by this.

Seek their wise counsel, not "tell me what to do." Webster's dictionary defines a mentor as "a trusted counsellor or guide." Mentors are not directors or managers of your life, nor are they parents. Rather they are people who are resources that you can draw from to achieve more than you can on your own. They are advocates for your life behind the scenes. Their goal is to help show you things that you haven't yet considered based on their own life experiences and to advise you on potential means to achieve what you want. They are not there to tell you, specifically and step by step, how to do something. They can guide you and give you direction, but the responsibility for the work still falls on you. They will not want to take credit for what you have done. They would rather help you position yourself so that it's all you.

With the guidance of a good and trusted mentor, you can have access to invaluable advice that will help you not only to stay on track and avoid veering off course but also to move forward in a more efficient fashion, with your eyes open even wider to the possibilities for your own personal situation. Good mentors will honestly and openly share their own experiences, successes, and failures with you so that you have the opportunity to learn from them.

When I was twenty-six years old, I landed a good job as a general accountant at a manufacturing company. Gary K., the CFO, became my mentor and taught me everything he could. I learned how to do complex balance sheet analyses, how to prepare tax returns, and eventually how to read and prepare financial statements. I became fascinated with the inner workings of a business and how to tell the story on paper through numbers. It was like reading a book to me, and reading was my passion.

I continued to take college courses, becoming more and more excited with the close of each semester and seeing more credits on my transcript. I did my homework anywhere I could, at lunch, at one or the other kid's ball practice, or in between games.

The company hired a new COO to make some changes. Steve B. was a barrel of a man who did not mince words. He came in like a tornado, making changes as fast as we could blink. I liked his fast pace and was not afraid of change. My whole life had been one change of scenery after another. He had a lot of different ideas that I was fascinated by. Steve challenged all of us to meet our full potential. "Belly up to the bar, folks!" he would say to us. Steve told me once that my CFO really wanted to promote me. The problem was that I wasn't approachable, Steve and Gary said.

They challenged me to work on my "social skills" and to tackle my weaknesses as a leader. "A leader?" I thought. I had never seen myself as a leader before. While my feelings were hurt at the criticism of my mannerisms, I allowed myself to cry over the disapproval for one night only. Then I decided to get up and try to make a focused effort to heed their advice and come out of my shell some more. I was aggressive on the inside about my own personal self-improvement, and they knew it. I just needed to let the rest of the world see the real me. It didn't take long for the moth to begin shedding its cocoon. Within six months of my review, I was officially promoted.

About two years later, Gary took me into his confidence one day. "Kim, I want you to stick to me like white on rice for the next few months. I am going to be leaving. The company can't afford a CFO with a salary like what I make. We need a controller, but you aren't quite there yet. I think I can get you there, though, if you'll commit to absorbing everything you can." I was saddened by his departure but thrilled at the future possibilities for myself. "I can do it!" I told him. And I did. Several months later, my teacher and mentor hugged me good-bye and said, "We'll keep in touch. You're going to do great. Keep working on your degree."

The following week, the company owner called me and congratulated me; he was promoting me to the position of controller, with the condition that I remain enrolled in college, working towards completion of my degree. I received a raise; while not exorbitant, it was more money than I had ever dreamed of making in my entire life. Had Gary and Steve not seen the potential in me and cared to take the time to be honest and help me develop, I would not have moved so far during that time. It set the foundation for the duration of my career, and I have always attributed my eventual success as a higher-level CFO to Gary and his mentorship. He remains there for me over twenty years later. One of the valuable lessons I learned from the situation with both Steve and Gary is that if you are going to reach your full potential, you must remain open to constructive criticism and not get stuck in a rut. This lesson served me well later in life.

Don't be afraid to reach out to potential mentors; they could help you unlock the untapped potential you have within or defuse the bomb that's just waiting to go off in your life because you do not even realize it exists.

Life is like rungs on a ladder. The reason they are placed so close together is so that we can learn to take baby steps and reach our destinations safely.

—Tom Baker, English Actor

Chapter 6
Baby-Step Your Way

How are you going to get to where you are going? Often the big picture can be intimidating. Your mission and vision for your life may seem completely out of your reach and unachievable at this point. You've done the work to break through the mental barriers and want to move towards bringing your dreams to life. Now it's time for action. You will begin by breaking down that big picture and establishing baby steps that, when taken one at a time, will eventually lead to your ultimate destination, bringing your mission and vision into reality so that you are living and breathing it instead of just imagining it.

It has been said that a journey of a thousand miles begins with a single step. Those small steps, laid out in advance and leading toward your ultimate goal, are the equivalent of a roadmap and your plan of action as to how to get there. Basically, these baby steps become your strategy. Without a clear strategy, you are likely to fail in your efforts.

> Small steps in the right direction are better than no steps at all, or worse, big ones in the wrong direction.

It's a known fact that only around 8 percent of goals set at each New Year are achieved. That's a 92 percent failure rate! You can't expect to get where you want with an inefficient, willy-nilly plan of action. Your goals can't be made in an abstract way. You've got to have a solid plan to bring them into the material world. When you get specific, things begin to materialize. Forming a strategy that will work for you is often one of the greatest obstacles to getting started.

If you aren't defining and then taking those steps, you are never going to get to where you want to go. Defining and documenting your steps and plan of action will lead to accomplishment.

So what are baby steps?

Baby steps are small, easily achievable parts of a larger objective. They are bite-size.

They will all vary, depending on what your specific intention is, how quickly you want to reach your ultimate, overarching goal, and how motivated you are.

Baby steps are the simplest and most effective method that you can use. You'll be achieving consistent small victories that you can build on, and this is the key to your overall success. The happiest and most successful people will tell you that their level of personal and professional success was accomplished by taking baby steps, making one positive choice after another in an effort to reach their destination.

Several years ago, my husband and two of his fireman buddies went on a safari to Africa. It was a dream for all three of them, and they worked for two years to put the trip together. When he returned, the pastor at our church asked my husband to speak at a conference and discuss how three average middle-class men were able to make such a trip a reality. Our pastor's goal was to explain to the audience that a person did not have to be wealthy to achieve some form of this goal. My husband's entire pitch was centered on the premise that you don't eat an elephant in one bite. You do it one small bite at a time and with patience, and that is how they prepared for and made this trip a reality.

Taking baby steps means you are in motion most of the time. This serves to excite and motivate you about your plan. It keeps you rooted in your commitment to achieve your goals, as you start to see immediate results.

The first step forward is to stop stepping backwards.

> Each time you are tempted to react in the same old way, ask yourself if you want to be a prisoner of the past or a pioneer of the future.

Set fire to the bridges that lead to the past habits that have been holding you back. You can't go back to your old way of life if you have destroyed the vehicle that will take you back there. It is the end of one era and the beginning of another. You can't just take a step into the future; you also have to eliminate the possibility of moving backward to the past.

That is how you go after your life-changing goals. That is how you break addictions, reconcile relationships, or get out of debt. To begin a new chapter, you must end an old chapter...no turning back. Failure can be settling for plan B when plan A gets too scary. Because of this, people often end up leading mediocre lives rather than the lives they dream of in their hearts. Burning the bridges to the past and breaking those old habits will keep you from backsliding and settling for mediocrity.

Spend some time in your journal listing any negative habits you have that don't contribute towards your new goals. Are you a procrastinator? Do you look for the easy way out of difficult situations that serves as a stopgap solution instead of working hard and finding the long-term cure? Do you find it difficult to open up and be vulnerable to criticisms that could benefit your behaviors and push you toward your goals? Do you become defensive when a trusted friend or mentor offers constructive criticism out of love for you?

What new habits that you didn't have in your former life will it take to reach your goal? What time do you need to get up each day? What do you need to do during the day? Do you need to set aside a specific block of time in order to work on it? Please write the answers to these questions in your journal.

When my husband and I decided to change our financial situation, we were deep in debt. We had to get a plan of action to eliminate the debt, then build our new foundation out of the right stuff. We educated ourselves on what it would take to get to where we wanted to go. First, we had to stop bad spending habits. We had to burn that bridge to the past. Just because we wanted something or because someone else had it didn't mean we were justified to buy it when we didn't really need it or, more important, could not afford it. Then we had figure out how to generate extra money and use it to pay off loans. We started with the smallest loan we had and paid it off. That one tiny step produced a positive result. It freed up the payment once allotted to that bill so that we could use it on something else. We used that money to pay off the second largest balance.

We took baby steps and were amazed at the residual snowball that developed. Within a year, we eliminated all of our credit card and installment debt, with the exception of our home and vehicles, and we had free cash flow to start saving. It created not only a sense of accomplishment and joy but also a sense of freedom that we didn't even know existed. It even improved our marriage, because we no longer argued about money. This burned another bridge to our past. We now had a "before" and an "after" to compare to, and there was never any going back for us. We were emptying our glass of dirt and filling it up, little by little, with fresh, crisp, clean water, and we did it as a team.

Mark Twain once wrote: *"If you eat a frog first thing each morning, nothing worse will happen to you the rest of the day."* I love what this symbolizes. The most difficult steps we need to take or the perceived hardest things on our to-do list are usually the things that we put off until last because we dread what we think it's going to take to get them done. The truth of the matter is that if we will just take the hardest step first, tackle it right away, and rip the band-aid off, then we know the worst is over, and it will get easier from there.

I struggle with eating the frog. I want to see constant achievement, and my frog of the moment makes me feel like I won't be accomplishing anything fast.

The frog in our lives, ironically, isn't the hardest thing to do; it's the item we dread doing the most or the volume of things creating stress in our lives. We build it up in our minds so that it becomes larger and more difficult than it really is. In reality, once we tackle it, we will realize that it was never as hard as we thought it was and was actually just a baby step in and of itself. I find that by not tackling the frogs in my life first, I am actually held back from accomplishing the most that I possibly can.

Eating the frog opens the door to productivity. The toughest thing in our minds is eliminated, and we can move on to the next.

This is a marathon, not a sprint, and we are going to finish this race by running one mile twenty-six times, not twenty-six miles once. If you can't run one mile, then you will need to break your steps down into half-mile or quarter-mile increments.

> All people on earth are running their own races.

You need to run yours in a manner in which you can achieve the vision you have set for yourself. Run in a manner in which you can win.

Setting short-term goals is important to get you started towards achieving the larger and overarching vision you have for your life. By doing this, you will start to see results immediately, which will motivate you to keep going. You will start to believe that what you have defined as the life you want for yourself is, indeed, achievable. Results will start to manifest themselves, and you will have something to show for your daily work.

Your short-term goals are subsets of the larger goal. They are stepping stones across the water to the other side. While you may not be able to see the other side of the river yet, you can set stepping stones close enough together that one step is visible from the next.

Use your journal to make a list of short-term goals that will enable you to move closer to your larger goal.

Be consistent with your work on these short-term goals. Make time in regular increments. This will help you form a habit and give you a greater likelihood of success, as well as keeping you moving forward in a regular, predictable manner. If time is an obstacle, please realize that even short durations can be incredibly productive. Working on one baby step for even fifteen minutes is better than not working on it at all. You can learn to be opportunistic with achieving your baby steps as well.

When I was still working on finishing my college degree, I was a busy stepparent with two small kids who had the typical busy schedule full of homework, T-ball, football, softball, dance, and so on. After work, my day extended to one practice or another, and, like most families, we didn't darken the door to our home until late evening every day. Many times at ball practice, I sat in the bleachers doing homework or studying so that I kept the ball moving forward on my education. I used the snippets of time I had and took every opportunity to work on a baby step towards achieving my goal.

Once you start setting small goals, taking baby steps, and working your plan toward your larger goal, doors will begin to open for you. If your goal is to have a successful career in a particular field, you can break down your baby steps into things such as taking one college course at a time, going to one seminar at a time, watching one webinar at a time, reading one book at a time, mastering one skill at a time, achieving one certification at a time, making one new contact at each event you attend, and slowly building your network.

As mentioned, baby steps will lead to doors opening for you. As a direct result of setting your plan in motion, you will have opportunities presented to you that are unexpected. In turn, you may find things moving faster than you anticipated.

> Your baby steps, as small as they may sound, are the jet fuel needed to get things off the ground.

One of the baby steps you might define for yourself is to talk to your mentors consistently. Keeping in touch with them regarding your plan of action will bring opportunity your way.

After my mentor Gary K. left the company, I stayed in my new position for a couple of years. The company was eventually sold to a larger company, which had someone already in my position. While I was asked to stay on in my existing role, I was dissatisfied at the lack of room for additional professional growth and did not want to stay idle with my career prospects. I decided to go a different direction, and I set a goal to go to work for a large public corporation, something I had yet to experience. I liked the idea of what skills I could add in an environment like that. I shared my plans with Gary K. throughout my initiative. I was successful in going to work for the largest publicly traded financial institution in the world at the time. One year later, I received a phone call from Gary K. He was helping a CEO find a CFO. "I think you are ready for this step," he told me. Indeed I was, and I landed my first CFO role at the age of thirty-two years old.

Taking a baby step and communicating to my mentor led to this door opening. While the personal and professional growth obviously happened, I was rewarded with significant financial growth at each of these steps as well.

Be consistent and build endurance towards this disciplined approach, and it will pay off for you.

Be patient; this is a lifestyle. Remain in the zone; make it part of your life. Keep it in the forefront.

> People who accomplish their goals do not have superhuman powers. They have persistence and a plan that they focus and work on every day until what they want to achieve comes to fruition.

Then, once they accomplish that goal, they set another. It becomes a lifestyle and a cycle of dreaming, acting, doing, repeating. Over, and over, and over again. It's a fluid situation.

Evaluate your progress along the way. This is important because it will motivate you to keep going. If you can see how far you have come, you'll know that it is possible to do more.

Take some time to write in your journal what you think you have accomplished so far. You'll find it useful later on to look back on what you've written and to remind yourself of the progress you have made during times you feel like things were going too slow or not moving at all.

Make adjustments when necessary, but do not stop. Don't fear growing slowly, but do fear standing still, or worse, stepping backwards. If you have circumstances arise that put a damper on what you are doing, then evaluate what's going on, where you are in your plan, and adjust your plan so that you are still moving forward. The next baby step may need to be broken down into two microsteps. That's okay, as long as you are still working on your plan and taking some sort of step to achieve your plan.

> Accomplishment will lead to intense pleasure, but failure is going to lead to even more intense pain.

When I was twenty-one years old, I worked for a college as the assistant to the dean of finance. She was a beautiful, fabulous woman whom I looked up to immensely. She insisted that I return to college as a requirement of my job. I was ashamed of dropping out of college years earlier and told myself frequently, "If you had stayed in, you would be finished by now." She helped me see that this was a damaging way to think and that it was doing nothing but holding me back from taking my first baby step in the right direction. She herself had married young, quit college, and not returned until she was divorced in her twenties. She told me, "Just take one class at a time and make it part of your life and routine. One day, you will look up, and you will be finished. Ten years is going to pass whether you are working on your degree or not. Wouldn't you like to wind up ten years from now with a bachelor's degree rather than looking back with regret?" She was indeed correct. I started with one accounting class on my lunch hour. From that point on, I took one class at a time for over ten years. I made education part of my life's routine, and it still is to this day.

I was thirty-one years old when I finished my first degree, which enabled me to move into my first CFO role at the age of thirty-two. I used the same method to earn a second degree and then to begin work on my master's degree. As I write this book, I am forty-eight years old. My goal has been to finish my

MBA by the time I turn fifty. I am blessed to have a very busy work and personal life, but years ago, I broke down my goal into reasonable, achievable steps mapped out over a period of time, and I strategically placed the courses I needed to take in order to finish. Why am I doing this? I have a successful career, but I have another goal. When I retire from the business world years down the road, I want to teach business courses at a university as a way to give back some of what I have learned through my career. I know that I need additional credentials to do be able to do this. Therefore, I've broken things down into steps, baby steps, and even microsteps.

Each day that goes past without action towards your goals only roots you deeper in your current set of circumstances. You have the power to change things now. You will need to do something every single day towards achieving your vision for your life.

Look back at the list of short-term goals you listed in your journal in the previous exercise. Choose one of those short-term goals you would like to accomplish. Make a list of baby steps and even microsteps, if needed, that are necessary to achieve this one short-term goal.

Great things are not done by impulse, but by a
series of small things brought together.
—Vincent Van Gogh

Wisdom is not a product of schooling,
but the lifelong attempt to acquire it.
—Albert Einstein

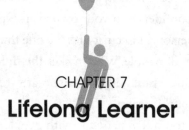

CHAPTER 7
Lifelong Learner

Let's take a moment, pause, and reflect on what we've accomplished so far:

1. We've become accountable for where we are, and we've begun to understand that we own and control whether we move forward and change our lives.
2. We've stopped making excuses and acting like victims.
3. We've established our personal mission, vision, and values that will guide us and serve as our road map moving into the future.
4. We've started thinking about selecting a mentor.
5. We've outlined baby steps in order to get started moving towards our vision. We have a plan.

Now we will explore the mind-set necessary to remain in perpetual forward motion for the rest of our lives.

> The most valuable thing you can take away from me is to become a self-educated person who never stops feeding your mind with new things.

It is the key to EVERYTHING I have ever accomplished. It gives you the power to "take it" instead of waiting for someone to offer it. It gives you confidence in your own ever-expanding abilities, and it destroys personal insecurity. It's the one thing that levels the playing field for all people. What makes the difference between those who are successful and those who aren't is whether they take advantage of this reality.

I don't have too much patience with people who think they can't do better because they weren't given the same opportunities as someone else. Even not being able to go to college is no reason. Everyone has access to the Internet and a public library. I notice an aura around people sometimes. I say people have "it" or they don't. "It" is the hunger and desire to improve yourself, not a desire for someone else to serve up an improved situation to you on a platter all nicely prepared, with fruit and cheese and real silverware on the side. I believe that you have "it." You only need to develop a conscious method of moving down the path to fulfillment and abundance.

You have some very unique talents. To not leverage them or to limit yourself to only what you are comfortable with now, out of fear of failure or getting out of your comfort zone, instead of expanding your mind to include things that will make you even more powerful, would be a waste of a good mind. My conversation with you is fueled from my knowledge *and* fear that you KNOW these things but might be afraid to use them in your own life. It does take courage, but as you get more confident, it will get less scary. If you understand what I am saying, this means that you have "it." It also means that you and I will both know that if you don't use that understanding to move forward, it will only be out of fear, and that would be a real heartbreak. If you stay on a path of continuous self-improvement, it will be something that begins to affect not only you, but those around you. It oozes.

You must commit to being a lifelong learner. What is lifelong learning? Quite simply, it is the ongoing, self-motivated, constant pursuit of knowledge for personal, spiritual, or professional reasons. It is the voluntary educational process by which people acquire knowledge, skills, habits, values, and attitudes. Self-proclaimed lifelong learners are motivated to learn because they want to. They have a hunger for it because they know the value it brings to their lives. It is a deliberate, desired act, which you totally control.

Knowledge is power, and it feeds your passions and your soul. It leads to deep delving, which leads to understanding not only yourself but your relationships, your career prospects, and your goals.

Knowledge and education about yourself and the world around you change the way you think. Changing the way you think changes the way you see things. Changing the way you see things changes the way you feel. Changing the way you feel changes the way you act and what you act on. Changing the way you act and what you act on changes your life. It's a cycle that produces continuous change and growth in your overall life. It sets things in motion and keeps them in motion. Winning people know how much they still have to learn, even when they are considered experts by others.

The most important thing you can ever do is to *learn how to learn* and then *never stop learning.*

It is necessary to thrive in life. Learning implies that you are constantly opening new doors, that you are are on a journey moving forward, and that your world is becoming enlarged. The most inspiring and empowering aspect of learning is that you are in charge of what you learn as a self-educated person, no matter the avenue you take to gain your knowledge and experience. Committing to never stop learning new things will help you understand the world you live in and provide more opportunities to improve your quality of life and achieve more. It constantly sheds light on the unknown or misunderstood.

Committing to lifelong learning is the equivalent of investing in yourself. You are the most important and valuable asset you possess. Investing in yourself will produce a return that is permanent and that cannot be diminished.

Learning for emotional development helps us learn about ourselves. This can be beneficial in identifying dysfunctional behavior that is standing in the way of us achieving our full potential. Our emotional intelligence will be strengthened as a result. We will learn to identify why we behave and react to things as we do.

American humorist James Thurber said, *"All men should strive to learn what they are running from, and to, and why."*

If you can continue to learn enough about what makes you tick on the inside, then you will be led to pinpoint the source of your self-worth and security. You need to be able to pinpoint your emotional triggers so that you can defuse your own emotional bombs.

One of my own emotional triggers is situations that cause me to fear not being able to take care of myself. The thought of it used to bring tremendous anxiety on me. Over time, I developed a sense of confidence, strength, and faith. With that growth came a sense of emotional intelligence that allowed me to recognize when I was being triggered into some sort of irrational response to my fears. I know now, and have known for years, that if I succumb to this trigger, I will not be able to inspire and motivate the people around me. It prevents me from looking outwardly to those who cross my path, and it ultimately keeps me from achieving my own definition of success.

Use your journal and spend some time focusing on identifying your own emotional triggers. Have there been instances where you have felt you reacted in a way that goes against the person you know you are inside? What about the situation made you react that way? Becoming more emotionally developed and in tune with your own psyche can help you challenge your own ideas and beliefs about yourself. Learning all you can about yourself can help you begin to see yourself in a more positive and healthy way. You will begin to understand what tools you possess to build on through lifelong learning that will help you in your journey.

Compare the journal exercise you just did to your entry earlier in the book, where I asked you to list negative thoughts you had about yourself, the LIES. How do you feel about that earlier list now?

Learning all you can about yourself, who you are, and why you do it will boost your confidence and self-esteem, as well.

> **Knowledge is power, and knowing yourself well is tremendously powerful.**

If you know and understand your own heart and mind better than anyone else, you will be less likely to fall into traps triggered by emotions that have no known origin to you. People won't be able to convince you otherwise in order to make themselves seem bigger or make you seem smaller. You will be less likely to allow others to derail your progress.

Behavioral and psychological assessments are a good method of educating you about yourself. They can bring to light the problem areas in your life and can offer valuable tools and help you learn more about what is driving your current reactions to things in your life.

Two of the most valuable profiles I have used were the Meyers-Briggs Type Indicator and Discover Your God-Given

Gifts. Both of these helped to bring things to the surface that I did not understand about myself. Traits that I possessed that I previously believed were negative were brought to light as critical parts of myself that could, when leveraged the correct way, be used to help me achieve even greater heights in my life. What was once perceived by me as quirks and negative qualities were in reality strong abilities that were merely manifesting themselves in my life in a negative and unhealthy manner. That is, I was using my real strengths in the wrong way, and the results being produced were negative instead of positive. For example, in addition to being ambitious, outspoken, aggressive, and driven, I am naturally gifted with a keen sense of discernment and perception. Mentally and emotionally, I am able to just sense things sometimes. Earlier in life, when I was less self-aware, when I sensed something with a situation or someone, I went on a warpath to fix it. I assumed that was what I was supposed to do if I had knowledge of it. I walked through life like a bull in a china closet, getting into things that were not any of my business and wreaking havoc in places I wasn't supposed to be in control of.

By educating myself about my own inner workings, I was able to learn how to get in tune with my own emotions, channel them in a more positive way, and use my unique abilities in a healthier way in my life and in ways that helped others. This type of learning on my part challenged the ideas and beliefs I once had of my own self and helped me to form new and healthy images of who I was. I gave myself permission to be me. That, in turn, only boosted my confidence and self-esteem, because I no longer beat myself up for who I truly was on the inside, nor did I allow others to beat me down any longer.

Learning for personal development will enable personal growth and uncover your hidden potential. Personal development insinuates that we, as people, can change for the better.

Personal development is a form of self-improvement and self-actualization, in which you start to actually become what you are capable of. You begin to achieve your full potential.

Because of the way I lived growing up, I was isolated more than normal from the usual social situations and groups of people. As a result, I entered the workforce as a young adult without ever really having developed a good sense of how people strategically maneuver around each other. Most people begin to learn this in high school and college, or younger. When I was in my early thirties and in a high-level management position, I realized that I was deficient in understanding the posturing that adults do with one another to get things done. I felt that my lack of awareness was a stumbling block for me. On one hand, it was nice to be so naïve, but the reality was that most people of the world I was working in *did* know how the game was played and I didn't. I shared this with a male boss, mentor, and close friend, who had a tremendous impact on my personal and professional growth. He was instrumental in helping me to elevate my way of thinking to a more sophisticated style, which enabled me to personally and mentally grow by giving me opportunities to be in situations that forced me to work on this aspect of my mentality. This growth catapulted me to a new level, both personally and professionally. Learning new things doesn't always come from books and reading. In this case, for me, it came from experiences I found myself in, conversations I had, and situations and people I had to learn how to deal with.

Spiritual development is a key factor in personal development. It is so important because basic trust is the foundation and it, therefore, helps develop and strengthen faith, which in turn helps us develop a solid sense of confidence by enabling us not to fear the future or the unknown. It provides a sense that your life is moving and evolving naturally, moving forward in a direction that may be uncomfortable but in a direction where we can be confident we will be safe. It can give you the confidence that the dreams placed in your heart are God-given and therefore coming from the right place and are meant to be.

> When you choose to believe in things that have not yet come to fruition, you have what is called faith. This enables you to tap into the power of what's possible. You are then in a position to overcome the past and the status quo.

As I continued to pursue my dreams, opportunities to experience new things continued to come my way. I began traveling and continued to be in positions I had not been in before, which was exciting but also scary. But my confidence in myself grew the more I traveled and faced new challenges in a normal world. As I trusted who I was becoming and my sense of self, I became even more empowered with regard to what I was capable of doing, and I truly began to believe that the sky was the limit.

Embracing change will always lead to you developing as a person. Change is naturally difficult for humans, but it is absolutely necessary for progress, and we must learn to welcome it. For some people who resist change, it is a matter of absolute laziness, but for others, it is the fact that they aren't in control of the outcome because it may be unknown. For you to change your life and move beyond the circumstances that exist for you now, there is no other way except to stir up change. Embrace it and have faith that things will work out as a result of the risk you are willing to take.

Learning to not fear failure is also key to personal development. You won't be successful with everything you try, but you will actually learn more from those situations in which you fail than you do from the home run events. Failure produces an opportunity to *learn*. Failure presents the opportunity to make the next decision informed, experienced, and full of confidence that you can succeed because of what you have learned. If you are committed to being a lifelong learner, you are inherently committing to be willing to fail, try, and fail again.

I am inherently a perfectionist. Getting things done and getting them done right is a big deal to me. However, I have been known to take this ethic to the next level and severely obsess about and beat myself up over failures. One of my dearest friends both personally and professionally has a mantra that says:

> We learn more from our failures than we do from our successes.

I think it's a great way of saying even our failures are successes if we learn everything we can from them. It's another way of saying we can always make lemonade out of lemons. The fruit of a tree is always out on a limb. The only fruit you get when hugging the tree trunk is the rotten fruit that has dropped to the ground.

Hard times do produce fruit in your life. My mother and I have discussed this in depth. I can honestly say that even though I have a life story that shocks and amazes some, I would not change anything. She agrees, although she adds the caveat that while she wouldn't change anything or what she has learned, we don't want to have to go through it again. We want to learn what we can from the difficulties and use those lessons to propel forward in life.

Open your journal and take a few moments to list some of your perceived failures. Next to them, discuss what you learned from the situation. Do the same with your perceived successes. Which were ultimately more valuable in terms of lessons to apply to the future, your success or your failures?

Learning for professional development will enhance your employment opportunities, which will, in turn, have a positive impact on your financial situation. Professional development opportunities can be situated in a variety of ways. While sometimes higher or formal education may be necessary, it is not always the case. There are so many means to learn new things for professional development in this day and age. Eliminate any excuse you may have. You have access to the Internet and a library, no matter what your financial position in life may be currently.

Learning hands-on technical skills by trying new things related to your particular field of interest can produce new levels of expertise in your professional life.

One of the many ways I learned new technical skills in my early professional life was to make a conscious effort to take something off my boss's desk every week. By doing that, I not only made myself valuable to my superiors; I was also reaching up instead of across and learning a skill that was necessary to reach a level higher than I was actually performing at the time. In essence, I was acting as if I had a position higher than my own anytime I took something off my bosses' plates and handled it. I became a go-to person for many people around me as a result of reaching to learn more. Eventually this began forming me into and positioning me as a leader, which I did not realize at the time.

While not always necessary, formal education may be required for you to take your life where you want it to go. Please do not let a perceived obstacle stand in your way of college education if that is what it will take to get you where you want to go. I made college part of my life, taking one class at a time for years and years in order to achieve my professional goals. (Remember: it is attainable with the right baby steps.)

Enhancing what you already know to grow where you are is another strategy to professional development. If you are a human resources manager for a small company that is growing rapidly, you will need to continuously improve your existing skills in order to remain the human resources manager when the company is twice as large. Strengthening and broadening your existing skills so that you are stronger, faster, more efficient, and more knowledgeable at what you do will provide development for you professionally as well.

What do you need to do? Take a moment to journal your list of goals. Then list the skills you need for each item and audit how ready you are to attain them. Where do you need to bolster your skills? List ideas on how you can supplement your knowledge in the particular area. How much time can you allocate to each new skills development? How can you carve out more time when necessary?

I developed a thirst for knowledge and continuous learning at an early age. It was a necessity. While my brother and I were living in hiding with our fugitive father, we missed a tremendous amount of school. There were entire years and grades that we missed. Many of the years that we did get to attend school under assumed identities, we only got to attend part of the year, as we would move from place to place around the country. At best, we had to attend multiple schools per year, sometimes as many as five in one year. This resulted in huge gaps in my book knowledge because of the time missed. Bouncing from school to school presented a different set of challenges, as each school's curriculum was different and one school might be at a different level than another.

Fortunately, I loved to read, and my dad encouraged it. While he did not allow us to watch television or listen to popular music, I always had access to a public library or a used-book store, where I could stay stocked up on books related to things I needed to know. This resulted in a very good literary knowledge for me, and I never struggled in English or history; actually, I excelled in these areas. Advanced math, however, was a different matter. I struggled tremendously with anything beyond basic math, such as algebra and geometry. I shied away from doing anything more than the basics to get by, because it was so hard for me and I was so afraid of failing. I was typically an A and B student, except when it came to higher-level math.

When I eventually started college, it was necessary for me to pass a standardized test to determine if I was ready for college-level algebra. I failed miserably. In order to be accepted into the program, I had to enroll in a remedial class to be taught what I should have learned in high school. Eventually, I was able to learn and gain the knowledge necessary to enter college-level math classes, but I was still weak in advanced mathematical concepts. The real challenge came when I went back to school in my twenties to earn a business degree in order to achieve my goal of becoming a CFO. Eventually, I mustered the strength to get through all of the math courses, and I earned my degree.

I was masterful at accounting and business and very confident and successful in these areas, but I still didn't completely understand the extremely high-level math concepts necessary to work in certain areas of the financial world. While I was doing fine and even excelling in my profession, I wasn't capable of going to Wall Street anytime soon, even if I had wanted to. Some of it simply just would not click with me. I knew I needed to do something to continue to learn more in the area of advanced mathematical concepts so that I could continue to grow not only upward, but outward, by expanding my radius. I found an online program that was not associated with any college, and I began the independent study necessary to get myself over the hump. It worked wonders for me, and one day, the lightbulb just went on. I was fascinated by what I had been missing. It reinforced what I already knew: if you work your brain, it will continue to get stronger, just like any other body part.

After this, so many new doors opened for me as my perceived opportunities multiplied. Eventually, I applied to and was accepted into an advanced MBA program and was able to successfully master the graduate-level finance and investment courses. Several years later, my career path also eventually took a new direction. I was able to use my past experience and improved skills to enter into the world of investing. I now source, make, and manage investments on behalf of high-net-worth people who trust me with their wealth.

As I mentioned, my new long-term goal is to teaching finance at a university one day, when I've retired from the corporate business world. I have only gained the confidence that this will be possible in the last ten years, as a result of challenging myself and finding creative ways to learn things that I was once weak in.

> **Don't believe or accept your perceived shortcomings.**

You are never too old, it's never too late, and you will never "arrive" at a place where it is okay to stop learning and developing. When I am dying, I will still be reading, learning, and growing to expand what I'm capable of. You can, too. If I can do it, anyone can. If I had accepted my perceived limitations with my math skills and fallen victim to an "I can't" mentality, I would have missed out on so many rewards in life. I would be missing out now. My return on investment has been over the top.

If you will motivate yourself to achieve education by reading and listening, you will see more and want to do more, unless you are complacent.

To each there comes in their lifetime a special moment when they are figuratively tapped on the shoulder and offered the chance to do a very special thing, unique to them and fitted to their talents. What a tragedy if that moment finds them unprepared or unqualified for that which could have been their finest hour.
—Winston Churchill.

NOTES

For every disciplined effort there is a multiple reward.

—Jim Rohn

CHAPTER 8
It's Worth It

How costly is it going to be to remain stuck where you are, in your current set of circumstances?

If you choose to remain in that warm cozy spot in that big pile of cow manure, it can cost you everything you ever dreamed of achieving.

Get out your journal where you wrote down all your dreams and goals earlier in this book. Feel it, hold it close to your chest, rub on it like it's a precious child. It can be a living, breathing thing if you don't give it up. Your words in ink on paper can become your life. Are you willing to trade that future possibility you are holding in your hands for what you're dealing with now? I'm begging you not to.

During the worst, most abusive part of my relationship with Ben, I became wrapped up in a vicious cycle of trying to convince him of the error of his ways, to be nice, to treat me right, and see things my way—all the while trying to do the right thing by moving myself forward. It was to no avail. We were making no progress. I began to get exhausted from the fighting and defending my motives. I was also becoming angrier with him by the day. I was not used to showing my anger, though. I was taught by my dad not to feel or express anger at the man in control of my life. I was taught to be submissive and endure whatever was decided by men and to believe that what they said was right. I knew that I was getting to a point where I could sink so low from the exhaustion and depression of the futile fighting to make things right that I would give up and this would become my life. I knew that in the battle between standing up for myself and the exhaustion and depression, exhaustion and depression were coming close to winning the war. I also knew that the way I was choosing to live my life was so far beneath what was actually possible. I was close to settling for less than what I deserved or wanted in life.

> It might be easier to just remain complacent, but it is not going to be worth it, *ever.*

You have two choices: you can change your life and move forward, or you can live with regrets about what could have been. You know it's possible. I know it's possible. Choosing to do nothing will produce nothing. Choosing to do *something* can produce everything.

There will be immediate and long-lasting benefits as a result of changing your mind-set and working on this program.

Things do not have to get worse than they are now—that is the immediate benefit. I have said this over and over as if I were a broken record, but it is absolutely true. Once the initial decision is made by you to consciously work towards your potential and destiny, the bleeding in your life stops, and you begin to repair and build on what you have to work with. It's a ticket to freedom, and the train is waiting on you to board it.

Momentum will start to build once you start making the mental, physical, and emotional effort. There is going to be some fuel in your tank to help propel you. You will be equipped to manage your emotions, understand their root cause, and overcome your fears. You will be happier and have more joy in your life, knowing you are overcoming your circumstances one day and one step at a time. Doors will begin to open for you that you were not expecting and will move you ever closer to your goal with more and more confidence.

By only living out of the memory of what has happened to you, you are dying.

> In order to be alive, you must live out of your imagination of what can be.

If you knew you could go to a casino in Vegas today, place a bet with everything you had in your checking account, and be guaranteed to double your money, you would do it. You cannot lose with this investment that I am asking you to make; it is a guaranteed win-win.

> You are choosing to invest in yourself, and that is going to produce a return that will compound and keep paying you back dividends forever into the future.

It will permeate every area of your life, affecting you financially, professionally, personally, and emotionally.

Doors will be opened for the right people to come into your life. The people you will then be surrounded with will strengthen you even further, helping you gain traction as you continue to grow and move forward. No longer will you be anchored, trapped, or held back by others who are small-minded or who are threatened by your potential.

It gets easier with the right support around you. If you have eliminated any toxic relationships that were holding you back or enabling your old behavior, you will then be open to new and healthy relationships that can strengthen you and support your journey. The right friends, mentors, and colleagues can inspire you, encourage you, and advise you, helping you stay on the right track. These people will help sharpen and hone you.

You'll gain new perspectives with mature, confident, and different influences in your life if you've surrounded yourself with people who care about your future and share similar values as you do. With fresh ways to look at things, your way of thinking will be broadened, and you'll see possibilities that you never knew were there. You will have finally emptied all of that dirt from your glass and have the space to fill it with clear and enriching water.

After I emptied my glass by leaving the unhealthy relationship I had remained in for years, I immediately sought out the right help for my issues. I went to counseling and started a twelve-step program for codependent people hosted by a local church. I was not interested in a serious relationship. There was no way I thought I could allow myself to dream of a man in my life. I was terrified of it. I cared about getting healthy and whole, then moving forward with my career and education. With my new lease on life, I was enjoying work even more. I had things I was doing for myself and things I was doing for others. I started to dream and plan what I wanted to do as my education progressed. I knew I had to have a vision of what I wanted my future to be. But God had more planned for me than I even had planned for myself. A mutual friend, who did not want to see me jaded about men for the rest of my life, introduced me to someone he proclaimed was "one of the nicest guys he knew."

"You just haven't met the right one yet," he told me. "You have been settling for less than you deserve."

I met Darrell, and he was the complete opposite of anything I had ever experienced. He was quiet, calm, and gentle, yet strong in every way that he dealt with me. He was a single dad with two small children, ages three and five. I had no idea at the time

that the day I met him was a pivotal point in my life. He had a
great work ethic, was also very driven himself, and was a huge
supporter of continuing education. He was also a good dad. He
was not controlling of me or anyone else. A healthy relationship
developed between us. I didn't feel any of the old, sick feelings.
I just felt safe with him and confident of his feelings for me. I
knew, from counseling, that I had to watch out for myself and my
triggers. I was also intent on not settling for less than what our
relationship could be. I fell in love with him and his two children
as a package deal. The work I had done through getting in tune
with my issues was key to this opportunity. I still wasn't perfect,
but I was aware and healthy enough to be grateful that Darrell
and his children came along when they did, and not a second
earlier in my life. We married after a couple of years. I had an
instant family with him and his kids. They had accepted me from
the beginning, and I adored them. I found I wanted to be a good
stepmother to children who needed me. With Darrell, I gained
a partner who supported anything I wanted to do. When I dove
back into college, he even tutored me and helped me study for
the algebra classes I struggled with. No one has ever been as supportive of and proud of me as he is to this day. Thanks to his son
and daughter, I learned what it feels like to be a parent. It was due
to the relationship with them that I made the effort to bridge the
gap with my own mother. I realized one day, when they were very
young, how painful it would be if, for any reason, my relationship
with them wasn't all it could be, and it showed me that I had to
do more to build the relationship with my own mother. Thanks to
these three, I learned what a healthy family feels like. The kids are
now grown. There have been graduations, jobs and promotions,
marriages and new babies. I can't look back on it all and not be
amazed. I have been a mother and a grandmother, two things I
would never have thought possible with the baggage I carried.

The contrast between this and the relationships I had earlier in life is so stark it is overwhelming. You can learn new things from a positive set of influencers in your life. You can learn not only how to do new things; you can also learn from other people's stories, mistakes, and successes. You can also learn to feel new things. You'll be in the circle of people who can help you achieve the vision you have for yourself and beyond. The natural benefit of this will be another means to continue your commitment to lifelong learning.

You'll be making an impact in the world yourself, once you are on the track to self-improvement. Positivity will begin to ooze out of you once you are in your groove, and other people will notice. Prepare yourself for people to begin seeking you out for advice, the way you have sought others.

The dime turns at this point. You will be giving rather than just taking what you need by making an impact and difference in the lives of those around you. This creates a residual effect, and a snowball starts to form.

You'll be turning into a change agent, not only for yourself but for others. Once you start the process in your own life and others begin to seek you out, you'll begin to share your story and what you have been through. You'll be planting seeds in the minds of others who want to bring positive change to their own lives.

You'll begin to put roots down that will lead to you leaving a legacy.

> You may not think you and your life are significant enough to make an impact on the world around you, but they are.

There is a theory that a butterfly fluttering its wings can produce tremendous and unanticipated outcomes in the world.

My younger brother was, obviously, also affected by what happened in our childhood. He struggled until he was almost thirty with finding stability and his own path forward out of the muck we grew up in. He was only six years old when our dad abducted us, and he barely remembered our mother. As a child, he was bullied in school a lot. As a young adult, he was somewhat transient and seemed to be struggling to find a purpose. While it took him time to find his calling in life, he eventually wound up finding his place as a firefighter and paramedic.

One day, after fifteen years on the job, he was called to a neighborhood to warn the residents about a natural gas leak. He parked his fire engine on the street and knocked on one door. An elderly couple answered, along with their three-year-old grandson. The little boy was shy and seemed scared. His grandmother explained to my brother that he was afraid of the fire engine and the sirens. After the firemen notified the other residents in the neighborhood of the leak, my brother returned to the house where the little boy was. He asked his grandparents if they would allow him to take the little boy out to the fire truck and show him around, to help him get over his fear of the fire engines and the sirens. They did, and the little boy had so much fun playing in the engine.

Later that day, as my brother was settling back down at the fire station, the grandfather showed up, looking for my brother. He and his wife had posted pictures of their grandson with the nice fireman on Facebook, where the little boy's parents saw them. The grandfather sought my brother out and said to him, "You know, that little boy you took time out of your day to play with today would not be here if it weren't for you. Neither would his older brother. Neither would their father." My brother told the man he was confused and did not understand. The man proceeded to tell him a story.

Fifteen years prior, when my brother was just a rookie, he responded to an incredibly terrible car accident on Interstate 35 in Dallas. A young newlywed couple had a blow out on the highway and had to pull over on the shoulder in the middle of the night to change the tire. While in the process of changing the tire, the young man was struck by an oncoming vehicle while his young wife was sitting in the car. He was severely injured, and it did not look like he would live. My brother resuscitated him on the side of the highway and kept him alive in the ambulance all the way to the hospital. He never knew whether the young man lived or not.

With tears streaming down his face, the little boy's grandfather told my brother, "That was my son, that little boy's dad. Because of you, he lived, and he and his young bride went on to have two beautiful boys. Because of you, we not only have our son; we also have grandchildren." The parents had recognized my brother on Facebook after all those years. Had my brother not started moving down a more positive path and made an effort to change and improve his life, he would not have had the opportunity to make such a huge impact in their lives. I'd say his efforts were definitely worth it. The kicker is that this is just one incident he was made aware of. How many more are there that he doesn't even know about? There is always a bigger picture that we cannot see.

We recently had a pool party and cookout at our home for a large group of friends. I was surrounded by my husband, my grown stepchildren, my son-in-law, my two grandsons, and about forty friends and their children. My younger brother was also there. As he and I sat together talking, he looked at me and asked, "Do you know all of these people here?" I told him that I did. He shook his head and looked around at our beautiful home and all the friends we were surrounded by. "Look at you. Just look at you. I'm so proud of you. Who would have ever thought that you would have all of this, considering where you came from?" Tears sprang to my eyes, because it was so true. There are moments like this that remind me of the magnitude of the journey I've been on and am *still* on to this day.

In order to paint the picture for you that my brother was referring to, let me take you to a small spot in rural Tennessee in 1980, where we ended up on our travels. I was ten, and my brother was seven at this point. My dad had found an old house way out in the country that needed a lot of work. We needed a place to stay, so he worked out a deal with the owners of the home to let us stay in the house in exchange for making the repairs it needed. To say that this house needed repairs is a drastic understatement. It had no windows and doors, no electricity, and no indoor plumbing. We slept on the floor and dealt with rats and other outside critters coming in the house. It was a shell. Our solution for a toilet that summer was a shovel to dig a hole in the field behind the house. We bathed with an outside water hose. We had virtually had no other human contact except each other. We planted a garden, and everything we ate that summer was grown ourselves. The house never got fixed up, and, after several months of "living" there, we moved on to the next place.

I remember that summer and compare it to my life now; I am first eternally grateful to the Lord for instilling in me an ambitious spirit willing to fight for my life and opening my eyes to the reality of my options. Second, I am always conscious of just how much all the effort was worth and how much it has paid off.

> To take the easy way out because it was simply easier would have been way too costly.

It would have cost not only me but also the other people who have been brought into my life that I've been able to be an example of what's possible.

We may never see the ripples of our positivity, but when we do, it's a beautiful testament to what is possible when we are present in our lives, striving for enrichment, and reaching out as the best versions of ourselves, regardless of our backgrounds that may tell us something different.

Treat others as you wish to be treated.
— The Bible

CHAPTER 9
Pay It Forward

Do you want to keep on achieving, obtaining more, and reaching heights you never dreamed possible?

Giving back by sharing what you've learned should become part of your life going forward. Once your eyes are opened to new possibilities in life through new ways of thinking and behaving, it's important to begin to help others by sharing your new knowledge. This enlarges the difference you are going to make in the world. You'll not only be improving your own life circumstances but also showing others how to do the same thing. You will come to represent possibility and positive change to those who cross your path.

Being a mentor to others, sharing what you've learned, and watching people you care about achieve their own success is incredibly motivating. They will serve as catalysts to inspire you to do even more with your own life, creating momentum so that you will never stop growing and your territory will continue to be enlarged.

The ones mentored will become mentors as you progress in your journey. I don't mean to say that you arrive at a place where you no longer need mentors yourself. You absolutely do;

however, you will begin to attract relationships with other people who need help.

People will begin to seek you out. This may surprise you at first, and it can be incredibly flattering and humbling at the same time.

Here is what Ann (age 50) has to say about our personal and professional relationship:

Kim and I started working together many years ago and almost instantly became very close friends. It was strange to me at first, because while we share the same values, we are very different as people. Kim has been my biggest influence and mentor professionally. She has patiently taught me so many things and has always tried to push me outside my comfort zone. She has taught, and is still teaching, me how to be strong around a group of powerful businessmen. Kim has also been a huge mentor in my personal life. She is always supportive and by my side. I have witnessed her teaching and mentoring many women, especially after major changes in their lives. She loves to help empower women so that they can support themselves if necessary. She has supported and encouraged women who have had drug addictions and who have suffered the loss of their husbands at a young age, and she has helped them get out of abusive marriages.

Over time, you should actively seek out opportunities to mentor others. In my own personal journey, once I learn something new, I am usually extremely eager to share it with someone whom I think it might make a difference to. Sometimes I can barely contain myself. It brings great joy to be able to provide a nugget that is just the little nudge that people need to help them get unstuck.

Here is what Deana (age 34) has to say about our mentoring relationship:

She is honest, she is blunt, and she is the friend and mentor that will tell you all the things you really don't want to hear. But, in order for you to grow and keep moving forward and succeed, you need to hear those things. There were times in my life that I honestly felt like I was not smart enough or able to do something, and Kim was always in my ear, pushing me along. Kim is encouraging and always working hard to build up others and make women better. Her story has been touching to me, because, so many times, you hear stories of people who don't overcome their struggles; rather, they let their circumstances become a crutch in their lives. Not Kim. She took the challenges that she faced and grew from them to be a very successful person. She wants to help anyone she can to better themselves. Kim and I have been friends for many years, and I am amazed every day at all of her accomplishments. She has played a huge role in the person that I have become in my career. I could not have made it this far without her pushing me and continuing to develop me along the way. I haven't always agreed with what she told me or liked what she said, but she is often right with the words she had to offer. I am forever thankful for our friendship along the way and all the support she has given me.

To be a mentor to someone else is an incredible responsibility but also one of the greatest privileges. When people go into this relationship with you, they are in need of something that they believe you have. They are trusting you with some part of themselves. You must be cognizant of this and have a plan to avoid hurting them. This is about them, not you. You need to be aware of what it will take to be a valuable and trustworthy adviser and counsellor. To earn respect and be worthy of a following, you need two qualities that really matter. First is conviction. By now, you should have developed a set-in-stone belief system that you live by and refuse to compromise at any time. There is a difference between steel and tin. Steel cannot be bent, torn, or crushed. Words of conviction sound like words of steel. Determined people have words of steel. This quality is important because if you don't believe in what you stand for and are trying to teach, then you cannot expect other people to buy into what you are saying.

The second quality of importance is credibility. People will listen to you if they trust you. To maintain the mentor relationship, you must demonstrate that you are reliable, have integrity, and are sincere. "Mediocre teachers tell, good ones explain, great ones demonstrate." We should strive to *be* the message, to walk the walk, and to talk the talk.

Here is what Denise (age 44) has to say about our relationship:

You really have no idea the comfort you can bring at the perfect time! Kim, every time I talk to you, I finally understand what my grandmother and mother tried to tell me my whole childhood! They wanted me to be independent, self sufficient, and a woman that would succeed. My grandmother had five children she raised on her own after her abusive husband died at an early age. My mother was in a management position for thirty years and always the breadwinner of my family. As I was the only girl in my family, they both begged me not to have a career and not stay home full-time with my kids. They meant well in doing so, but that's not where the Lord was leading me. I have seen the fruits of my labor in staying home but thought it was time to go back to work after being a stay-at-home mom for over twenty years. I picked a consuming career choice, and I haven't been able to figure out how to balance between work and family. I didn't have role models to show me how to balance both. But I have now realized that my mother and grandmother HAD to work the way they did to survive! Every time I talk to you in general, I walk away feeling like there IS a way to balance the madness of businesswoman, wife and, mother! You did both, and you give me a clearer understanding that my true desire is actually possible. Talking to you brings me hope and a healthy confidence in myself to continue to strive for that healthy balance. You are the real deal, sister, that brings hope and light to a dark world. Your speech and the way you word things just make sense! You deliver it in a way that makes other women look to you for guidance. I pray you continue to encourage others as you do me!

Kelly (age 25)

Time and time again, I've heard people say that you can only count on yourself to get you where you want to be in life, but I think there are some places that are just out of reach without the help of someone else—whether that help is to point out a different route, to lift you up to the next level, or anything in between. Sometimes those people are friends or family, but a lot of times, those people are your mentors. The definition of a mentor is "an experienced and trusted advisor." Kim was my mentor, and while that definition certainly does apply, she was, and is, so much more to me. She's been the person to point out different, and often better, routes, to lift me up, and to give me something to lean on. She's become not only my mentor and my friend but also someone I consider family. When I met Kim, I was still what I would consider barely into the world of accounting and, in a lot of ways, the professional world in general. Fortunately, I also had another amazing mentor earlier on who had taught me all the fundamentals of accounting. When I started working with Kim, I was initially intimidated because she was someone that I could easily look at and know that that was where I wanted to be one day in my career. Not only was she smart and professional; she was also kind and very respected—all things I aspired to be. We worked together for probably a year, when I learned not only how to do such a large number of things beyond what I even realized I didn't know but also how to take constructive criticism, how to be more professional, and especially more about her. The things I learned about her confirmed that initial thought I had—that that was what I wanted to be one day. I had struggled for what seemed like a long time to find what it was that I felt like was my "calling." Through working with Kim and my first mentor, I knew that accounting was that place for me. Going back to school for accounting was a decision that I was toying with. I knew that I would need a degree to be able to get where I wanted to be one day. I was scared that I wouldn't be able to do it again, now that I was "past the normal college student age." Once I decided that I was going to do it, I told Kim, and I will never forget that day. I expressed both my concerns and my excitement to her. She told me her story and how she hadn't taken the traditional route through her career, either. She told me that it doesn't matter when you find that place, just that you do, and that the time is going to pass regardless, so I might as well use every day to the best of my ability and pursue the career that I actually wanted. Now I'm one semester away from being eligible for the CPA exam, and there is no doubt in my mind that Kim, her mentoring, her friendship, and her advice contributed a huge amount to my success. Besides teaching me and motivating me, Kim has done more for me. I was going through a rough patch and struggling with what to do next in my career—big choices for a twenty-three-year-old. She helped coach me through the decision to take the next step in my career. By helping coach me, I mean that she helped me come to the decision that was right for me, helped me update and properly format my résumé, helped me learn and prepare for interviews, helped me find recruiters, and taught me how to navigate the scary world of job searching. She even took me shopping for a starting "business professional" wardrobe. She was there to pick me up when I had lows and there to celebrate my successes with me in my highs. Fast forward to this current day, years later, I'm still leaning on her for support and learning. She's helping me learn and practice extra things to advance in my career, and she's still helping me navigate through what I even want for myself.

Along the way, Kim has always told me that when I get the chance, I need to pay it forward. She also had amazing mentors who helped her learn when she needed that. I look forward to paying it forward because I see in so many things what she has done for me—both personally and professionally. I've heard the stories of her mentors and how important those people were to her and how she gives them credit where credit is due for the role they played in her life.

I want you to develop a healthy attitude about yourself and your story. I don't want you to forget where you came from. I've said, from time to time in this book, that you cannot get complacent and that I do not think that you will finally arrive at your destination and get to stop moving forward. You can stop for a moment, from time to time, and celebrate your latest accomplishment, but you need to continue to move forward.

At the same time, as you remember where you came from, it will help you protect yourself against a prideful attitude. This will ensure you attract the right opportunities to give back what you have received.

When I ran away at sixteen, I took a flight alone to Dallas. My aunt was supposed to be waiting for me at the gate. I couldn't believe what I had done. I would have never thought I would have the desire or capability to walk away from my dad. I felt strangely calm and at peace with what I was doing. As I stepped off the plane and into the gate, I realized she was not there. I found myself alone, wandering around. I was terrified she had changed her mind and I was going to be stuck there, with all of ten dollars in my pocket. I remember walking through the terminal in my ragged jeans, T-shirt, and tennis shoes, with one duffle bag that held all my possessions. All of a sudden, I saw her power-walking down the aisle toward me. I was so relieved to see her! Even though I felt like I had done the right thing, I had never been so scared or felt so alone. Over the years, I have found myself at that same airport and same gate, departing for a business trip, looking polished and sporting designer shoes and a bag that I never would have dreamed of owning. I never take for granted how far things have come. The memory hits me like a wrecking ball every single time I am there, and I am overwhelmed with gratitude and humility at how different my life is. It is not merely the material stability, but, much more so, the sense of well-being and confidence that I have. But, above of all, it is gratitude—gratitude for the loved ones and overwhelming support that I have in my life. I never take for granted the success I have had, having started out in a place in life with other people, people that I loved, telling me I wouldn't, couldn't, shouldn't be all that I dreamed of being… things they did not want to be or could not be themselves.

Gratitude is an important part of paying it forward. This feeling is born out of remembering where you came from.

> If you are grateful for the opportunities you've had and all that you have learned to help you out of your former circumstances, it produces a desire to pay something back.

Remember your own mentors. Remember when you wanted what you now have.

Spend some time in your journal and reflect on your achievements along your journey. How do you feel about what you have attained in your life thus far? Imagine the advice you would have given yourself in the past to even better ready yourself to be where you are now. How have your perceptions of your goals changed now that you are living the reality?

Humility is important. Remain confident in your abilities and self-worth, but don't get proud and overly cocky. It's important to not display an air of superiority to the rest of the world. The image you want to project to those you mentor is confidence and one of "if I can improve my life, anyone can."

As I progress in my journey, stewardship has become more and more important to me. I want to be sure I spend this life and my time in the most valuable way in order to create the greatest residual reward and return for myself, and ultimately for others. I learned to consider how I was using what I was given (time, money, etc.) from a very wise woman in my life.

"We are here on earth to help others." Period. The same very successful and generous woman once told me this. We can make the most impact if we take care of and cultivate what we have ourselves.

> Get yourself to the point where you are able to be a light to others. You can't do that if you remain where you were when you started this book.

While I have always wanted to be an inspiration and mentor to many other women, there is one young woman I have cared most about being a good influence to.

Courtney (age 28):

Kim has been in my life since I was a little girl, when she married my dad. My brother and I were part of the deal. She has never treated me as anything less than her daughter. She has always pushed me to set my goals high and work hard to achieve them. I have seen her go through highs and lows, but, through it all, she stuck true to herself and kept her head held high. She has come a long way in her life. Even though she may now be a successful woman, she never judges others when they are down. At times in my life when I have failed, I have worried that I may disappoint her. But instead of being upset, she picks me back up and motivates me to keep going. I know that as I have continued to grow, both professionally and personally, her confidence and drive has rubbed off on me. That will help me become a better, more successful woman.

Be healthy. Be authentic. Be open. Share your story. It was given to you for a reason, and that reason is not to tuck it away in your mind and heart. It is your story to tell, and you need to tell it. It exists so that you can use it to help other people. It is a very valuable commodity that you have, and it should not go to waste, and you should not be selfish with it. I have always felt an obligation to share my story. It has come easy for me, but it doesn't come easy for everyone to talk about things that may be private, personal, shocking, or embarrassing. Once you have benefited and gained wisdom from it, be willing to share it and give a piece of yourself to those in need.

Take some significant time to write your story in your journal from your perspective. Where did you start in life? What is your family history? What has happened to you over time?

You should have no embarrassment or shame. Shame hurts and floods your mind. You can turn that faucet off whenever you want. Own your situation and embrace it.

> The most courageous thing you will ever do is to own your story.

You can leverage whatever has happened to you so that it turns into a tool to help others, if you open yourself up to being used as proof. You can become a beacon and a light to say to others, "Anything is possible."

Determine what you stand for, then craft your message. Use the values you defined for yourself in your journal earlier in this book. Hone your words of steel. Look back in your journal to the earlier entry where you wrote about who you are.

What lessons do you now have to offer? What can others learn from your experiences? Write these answers in your journal.

While owning your story takes courage, once you embrace it and accept the responsibility to share it, use good judgement when choosing your audience. Be smart when choosing the time and place in which to share your message. With maturity and wisdom comes discretion, and depending on what your past includes, you may need some education and advice on the right ways to share what you've been through. This is important because while I want you to share your story to make a difference, I don't want you to expose yourself to people who may take advantage of the knowledge they have about your past. There is a time and place for everything.

You need to figure out who your audience is and not cast your pearls before swine, so to speak. I will give you an example: If you are a victim of sexual abuse, you would want to be careful about sharing your story in a room full of men that you don't know. You may be better off seeking a group of women who are in need of hearing your story. I learned this from a close male friend and mentor once, when I decided to share part of my story I had harbored for many years. "Be careful who you share this with, Kim," he commented. "There is a time and place for everything. You could tell this to people who would take advantage of you." Choosing your target audience wisely in certain cases can be key to giving back effectively and producing the biggest impact.

STUCK

Spend some time thinking about who needs to hear what you have to say. Make a list in your journal of individuals or groups with certain qualities or issues who could benefit from listening to your story.

Help enough people get what they want
and you will get what you want.
—*Zig Ziglar*

You have been created with the ability to change the world. Every single choice you make…every single action you take matters. But remember, the converse is also true. Every choice you do not make…every action you do not take … matters just as much.

—Andy Andrews

CHAPTER 10
Conclusion

I am so pleased that you stuck this out. You are now equipped with some tools to overcome adversity that have worked well for me. You have learned that YOU are in control and YOU get to decide not only your actions but how you focus your thoughts. These are powerful tools that will serve you well in all that you do going forward.

We have come so far on this journey of transformation and worked hard to grasp the mental strategies necessary to surpass your circumstances and position yourself for never-ending momentum towards meeting your full potential in life. You have worked with determination to make the mental shift from victim to overcomer.

We began with facing the cold hard facts that no matter where you started in life or where you find yourself now, you are in charge, and there is no excuse for not making the effort to turn things around, do something successful with your life, and become a person who adds inspiration and value to those around them. The choice is simply yours. It may be overwhelming at first, but you now understand how much power is in the shift.

We have faced our circumstances, taken responsibility for where we are, and eliminated any victim-like mentality. We understand that it may not be our fault that we are where we are, but it is our fault if we remain stuck.

We have destroyed negative thoughts and removed any lies hiding inside us that are holding us back. We will not allow ourselves to remain downtrodden and stuck in a pit of despair. We will allow ourselves our emotions but will not be controlled by them.

We eliminated "I can't" from our vocabulary and began looking at what's really possible. We stopped being lazy and decided to take action. As a result, we faced the fact that we are going to have to become comfortable with change and face our fears. We acknowledged that we may have become complacent and were feeling warm and cozy in our own big pile of cow manure. We now know that in order to have the good things in our life that we dream of and were intended to have, we must first empty the dirt out of our glass and prepare ourselves for filling it back again with fresh, clean water.

We ignited a passionate desire to achieve the things we are dreaming of and became excited about taking the right next steps forward—all the while knowing that anything worthwhile will not come easy.

We've searched our heart and soul for buried dreams and ambitions and rekindled old flames that have flickered out. We then set concrete goals around what we want to do, as well as defined our personal mission, vision, and values. As a result, you now know what you stand for. We've developed a road map, and we've begun our journey forward towards a life of achievement.

Take some time to revisit your journal exercises and recap your new mission, visions, and values. How does it feel to have a concrete sense of purpose that you developed yourself?

We've learned to act and think as though we already have what we are trying to accomplish. We've torn down any sense of insecurity or thoughts that we don't deserve better. We've studied how to think and act like what we want to become. We will no longer think that other people are better or more deserving than us. We are committed to doing what we need to do to get ourselves from where we are to where we see ourselves in our mind's eye. We have learned to act happy in the face of our adversities and to understand this alone will serve to bring a sense of positive change to our lives. We have decided not to settle for mediocrity in our lives.

We've discovered that having mentors in our lives will bring an incredible sense of stability to what we are trying to do and will help validate and hold us accountable when necessary. We now know what we should be looking for in mentors, and are not embarrassed by anything that has happened to us in the past. We are open to sharing our failures with trusted advisors in exchange for valuable input and guidance.

We have realized that the key to getting where we want to go is just to start, take the first step, and continue taking baby steps forward. We didn't get into trouble overnight and won't get out overnight, but we can stop allowing our lives to stand still, or worse, erode even further. We know that things do not have to get any worse than they are now.

We have a clear understanding that this is a lifetime commitment and that we must continue to stretch our minds and learn new, foreign things. Education changes the way people think; therefore, we are dedicated lifelong learners who will never stop thirsting for more knowledge and wisdom. We will continue to develop channels in which to educate ourselves towards our goals. There is always a bigger picture than what we can see at the level we are at. The sky has no ceiling, and neither does what we are capable of learning. The only way to continue to gain a new perspective of the world around us is to continue our commitment to gaining knowledge and educating ourselves. Wisdom will produce fruit in your life; it leads to truth. The opposite is folly, which is full of lies. Wisdom and knowledge protect you against vulnerability.

While we know this will not be easy, we realize that our eyes are opened and that to not act on our new understanding would be sheer laziness and poor stewardship of the talents we have been given. We know that this will be worth the effort that it takes. It is clear that doing nothing will only lead to regrets. Time is passing whether we move on what we know or not, so we might as well start the process and move forward one step at a time.

All of our newfound wisdom, knowledge, and success will dovetail into the ultimate reward. As we begin to pay it forward, we will realize the reason we worked so hard. We will realize our real purpose in life is to help others through being the best we can possibly be and then sharing our story and journey with them. We begin to see our impact on others as we learn to be mentors ourselves. We did not do all of this for selfish gain. We worked and will continue to work so that we can be a light shining bright to others and a beacon of hope as to what's possible. We will help others learn what we've learned. We have watered and cultivated our own garden and will continue to do so, but it is also now time to plant seeds in other places. Wisdom, knowledge, and education will lead you to call on others. You will want to help strengthen the vulnerable and open their eyes to another way of life.

We know that we will have moments of failure. These times will be used as lessons to strengthen us and to use as reference points in the future, as well as to help others we mentor. Our failures will not, however, be permanent, nor will they be enough to get us off course. They will provide valuable learning opportunities. At times we may take a step back, but after we take three steps forward, the net result is still positive. Even if you lose ground at times or backslide, you are changed for the better and will have the ability to pick up and continue to move forward towards your vision. The thought of giving up will now scare you, because you now know what you will be losing. You've had a taste of success, and you have something to compare and contrast to. Your eyes have been opened. You now know what you will be missing if you regress at this point.

While you may currently be enmeshed in your circumstances, the future is now bright. You know that things will not get worse. You have what you need to start progressing with positive change in your life. Here is the kicker:

> It is now impossible, IMPOSSIBLE, to return to the place you were when you started this book. Life has literally changed with your eyes being opened, and you are empowered to do something about your circumstances.

You have what you need to move into action and turn this life of yours around. You will begin to see results immediately, and that will give you the motivation and desire to continue. You are empowered and strong enough to take the next step and the next. Your confidence and self-worth will continue to strengthen as you move on. You will be able to identify negative influences in the future that may be stumbling blocks to your progress. You will be able to consciously surround yourself with people and situations that feed your growth, and you will eventually be a presence to others and fuel their growth. You will grow from helping others grow.

You will be better tomorrow than you are today, and better the next day than you are tomorrow. You will work hard but, with the positive effects being produced in your life, you will begin to feel a sense of accomplishment and satisfaction that will prevent you from going back and picking things up from the past. While your past will serve as a foundation and something to learn from, it will not control you or the outcome of your life. You will continue to overcome adversities that arise in the future.

Other people will begin to seek out your advice and expertise. You will, as a result, begin to mentor others. As you impact others over time and they move forward and use what they have learned to mentor others, a domino effect occurs. You will leave a legacy that will impact many people who cross your path, some of whom you will never meet or know about.

The next steps you take are important. Don't let what you've learned go stale and stagnant. Take immediate steps to put into action what you have learned over the course of reading this book. Go back through the journal you've been keeping as we worked through all of these steps. Allow yourself to see the difference in your thinking from when you started to now. This will reinforce and validate what you've learned. Begin with what you are not going to do any longer. You are not going to believe that what you want for yourself is impossible. Every day tell yourself, "I'm possible."

Look back in your journal at the list of lies in the past that you had once told yourself. Do you still believe them?

Develop your own personal mantra that inspires you. This can be a passage from Scripture, a quote, a song, a poem, or something you write on your own. Play it over and over in your head. Write it down in your journal. My own personal mantra reads: Strip off every unnecessary weight and run with endurance and perseverance the race that is set before us (Hebrews 12:1).

> You will need to run your own race with persistence. Growing into the fullness of the person you are intended to be will take time. However, you can enjoy each step of growth along the way, if you choose to.

Put a smile on your face every day and act as though you are happy. If you don't really feel happy, make a conscious effort to find something around you to smile about.

If you find it necessary, begin taking steps to eliminating negative and unhealthy relationships from your life. Seek out professional counselling if you need to.

Talk to a trusted friend. Look at your goals and decide what you can do to start moving towards them. Buy a new book on the subject, attend a seminar, or register for a college course.

If your goals are around your professional life, for example, look at your clothes and determine if you are dressing for the job you want or the job you currently have. If you are dressing for the job you currently have, then buy some new things and start dressing for the part you want to play. If your goals are personal in nature, are there new habits you need to form or old ones you need to break in order to take the first step forward?

Look around you and see who is doing what you want to do. Who has already accomplished what you envision for yourself? Try to make connections with someone and bring a mentor into your life. You'll be surprised how many people will want to help you move forward.

Spend some time journaling specific next steps in your journey.

My commitment to you has been to offer tough, honest, yet encouraging words that will help you clear the cobwebs of discontent and insecurity. Hopefully your mind is open to the possibility that you can do something with what you have, no matter where you are now, where you came from, what has been done to you, or what mistakes you have made. I want you to believe that you can be your own possibility.

I have walked you through the ups and downs of my own journey with true stories of sadness, hope, failure, and success. I have shared with you my "cloud nine" moments, my "aha" moments, my "oh crap" moments, and all the good, bad, and ugly. But in the end, this is a story and a lesson of faith and mental strength, learning how to stand your ground and fight for yourself, and how to be responsible and accountable for your own outcome. You have learned how to stand on your own two feet. We all have free will and can choose how we are going to respond to what has happened and how we are going to use what we have learned. We each choose our own attitudes. This we are in control of.

I am incredibly proud of you and the journey you are about to embark on. I am honored and privileged to have had the opportunity to walk with you and share my story, and I am humbled that you took the time to listen. I can't wait to see what you accomplish in this life! You are your own possibility, and achieving your potential is only a matter or starting, working hard, remaining faithful, and believing in yourself.

Allow me to share one final personal entry from my own journal:

Dear Past: Thank you for your lessons.

Dear Future: I am ready.

Dear God: Thank You for another chance.

Not all storms come to disrupt your life. Some come to clear your path. Forgive yourself for not knowing what you didn't know before you learned it. Have no regrets. You are never too old to start over, to set another goal, or to dream a new dream. Within you is the power to rise above any situation or struggle and to transform into the brightest and strongest version of you. Move on and be your own possibility!

There will come a day when you will look back and remember when you once wanted what you now have. When that day comes, allow gratitude to wash over you, then set a new bar for yourself, kick things into high gear, and move on again.

Overcome, my friend. You are worth it, and the world needs you and all that you have to offer.

About the Author

Kim Casey Cobb makes her home approximately one hour south of Dallas in Corsicana, Texas. She began her career in business in her early twenties and served much of the last two decades as a chief financial officer in various industries. She currently serves as an advisor to business owners and works in the investment community. She holds a bachelor's of business degree in business and has attended the Graduate School of Texas A&M University Commerce. Kim is happily married to her husband of over twenty-three years and helped raise two stepchildren who are now grown. She has been an avid marathon runner and has completed the New York City Marathon three times. She enjoys traveling, reading, writing, and mentoring others.

To book the author for a speaking engagement, event, book signing, or mentoring session you may contact her at:

www.kimcaseycobb.com   Contact Us
email: kcobb@ebspartner.com
Mail: 3701 NE CR 0120   Corsicana, TX   75109